# Self-Confidence for Men:

*Unleash the Lion within and See How Your Mental Toughness, Self-Esteem, Mindset, Self-Discipline, and Dating Life Transforms*

© Copyright 2020

The contents of this book may not be reproduced, duplicated, or transmitted without direct written permission from the author.

Under no circumstances will any legal responsibility or blame be held against the publisher for any reparation, damages, or monetary loss due to the information herein, either directly or indirectly.

Legal Notice:

This book is copyright protected. This is only for personal use. You cannot amend, distribute, sell, use, quote, or paraphrase any part of the content within this book without the consent of the author.

Disclaimer Notice:

Please note the information contained within this document is for educational and entertainment purposes only. Every attempt has been made to provide accurate, up to date, and reliable information. No warranties of any kind are expressed or implied. Readers acknowledge that the author is not engaging in the rendering of legal, financial, medical, or professional advice. The content of this book has been derived from various sources. Please consult a licensed professional before attempting any techniques outlined in this book.

By reading this document, the reader agrees that under no circumstances is the author responsible for any losses, direct or indirect, which are incurred as a result of the use of the information contained within this document, including, but not limited to, —errors, omissions, or inaccuracies.

# Contents

INTRODUCTION ..................................................................................... 1
PART 1: SELF-ESTEEM ........................................................................... 4
SELF-ESTEEM AND WHY YOU NEED IT ............................................. 5
    WHY YOU NEED SELF-ESTEEM ....................................................... 6
    CONSEQUENCES OF LOW SELF-ESTEEM ........................................ 7
    ASSESSING YOUR SELF-ESTEEM ...................................................... 8
    DETERMINING YOUR SELF-WORTH AND PERSONALITY ............ 9
    YOUR SELF-ESTEEM ANALYSIS ...................................................... 11
OVERCOMING INSECURITIES AND SELF-DOUBT ......................... 12
    CAUSES OF SELF-DOUBT ................................................................. 13
    EFFECTS OF SELF-DOUBT ................................................................ 14
    SIX EFFECTIVE REMEDIES FOR OVERCOMING SELF-DOUBT ... 14
    SELF-DOUBT TEST ............................................................................. 18
    TEST ANALYSIS .................................................................................. 19
    BODY IMAGE: HOW IMPORTANT IS IT? ........................................ 19
    FEELING GOOD ABOUT YOUR LOOKS .......................................... 21
    HOW DO YOU KNOW YOU HAVE BDD? ........................................ 23
EVEN MEN NEED SELF-LOVE! ............................................................ 26
    THIRTEEN HABITS TO PRACTICE IN ORDER TO DEVELOP SELF-LOVE ........... 27

THIRTEEN SELF-ESTEEM HABITS TO PRACTICE DAILY ....................... 33
PART 2: SELF-CONFIDENCE.............................................................. 39
SELF-ESTEEM VS. SELF-CONFIDENCE ......................................................... 40
    TEN INDICATORS OF CONFIDENCE .................................................................. 41
    SELF-CONFIDENCE TEST..................................................................................... 42
    MAKING YOURSELF THE PRIORITY ................................................................... 46
    FIFTEEN PROVEN WAYS TO BOOST YOUR SELF-CONFIDENCE........................ 47
LIKE A BOSS: SIX WORKPLACE CONFIDENCE HACKS ........................ 53
    THE SIX WORKPLACE SELF-CONFIDENCE HACKS ........................................... 54
DATING CONFIDENCE: TWELVE IRRESISTIBLE STRATEGIES TO WIN HER OVER ....................................................................................................... 59
TAMING YOUR OVERCONFIDENCE ......................................................... 68
    TEN HABITS NECESSARY FOR TAMING OVERCONFIDENCE ............................ 70
PART 3: SELF-DISCIPLINE............................................................... 74
SELF-DISCIPLINE AND ITS CORE VALUES................................................... 75
    SIX REASONS WHY YOU NEED SELF-DISCIPLINE............................................. 76
    WHY MEN LACK SELF-DISCIPLINE ................................................................... 78
MINDSET MATTERS: CHANGING YOUR LIMITING BELIEFS ................ 80
    THREE BAD MINDSETS THAT YOU SHOULD AVOID ........................................ 81
    SEVEN WAYS TO DEVELOP CONFIDENCE WITH THE RIGHT MINDSET ........... 82
    MINDSET SELF-TEST .......................................................................................... 85
    MENTAL TOUGHNESS: THE ZERO F*CKS METHOD .......................................... 86
    SKILLS THAT DEFINE A MENTALLY TOUGH MAN ............................................ 87
    ROUTINE HABITS OF MENTALLY TOUGH MEN ................................................ 89
FIVE SELF-DISCIPLINE HABITS FOR DAILY IMPROVEMENT ................ 93
    POWER GOALS: THINKING LONG TERM FOR SUCCESS ................................... 98
BONUS – TOP TEN TIPS TO BE A CONFIDENT MAN ........................... 104
CONCLUSION............................................................................... 106
SOURCES ..................................................................................... 109

# Introduction

It doesn't matter what your background is; you can develop self-confidence. This book contains proven strategies that will teach you how to boost your confidence, establish lifelong self-esteem, conquer self-doubt, and enhance your self-discipline. When you finish reading this book, these things will no longer hold you back. You will genuinely believe in yourself, and you will reach your full potential.

Self-confidence is a mighty force within you. It affects your success at work, with your family, and in relationships. The purpose of this book is to unpack this force and present it to you in a concise, easy to comprehend manner. It is suitable for everyone—all ages, men, women, coaches, employees, students, adolescents, and of course, you.

This book will lead you down the path of believing in yourself, which is the essential asset you need in your life. Riches and fame cannot be substitutes for a lousy self-image. Lack of confidence will always hold you back and make you under-achieve. Additionally, low self-esteem often leads to divorces, horrible parenting, relationship problems, drug abuse, unemployment, poverty, et cetera. If you are a victim of any of these, then buying this book is the wisest thing you have done for yourself. The impact of the lessons in this book, if followed religiously, are permanent and will transform your life for good. You will notice a tremendous change in your confidence in less than two months.

Unlike other related books, the strategies in this book are very practical and have been carefully structured to assist you in building your confidence, self-esteem, and self-discipline quickly. However, to benefit from this book, you will have to do more than just read it. You must do the proposed exercises in the book. For example, if you are requested to take a pen and paper to do something, you should take a pen and paper and write as advised.

Here, we will use proven methods of cognitive-behavioral therapy to increase your confidence by changing how you interpret your life. We will use easy steps to uncover and analyze negative self-statements that you probably make. We will also teach you how to create new goals in life and make positive self-statements that will foster your self-confidence—as opposed to undermining it. This book will equip you with the necessary skills to squash doubt and substitute it with confidence.

This book focuses entirely on taking action. It contains proven steps and strategies on how to identify that low self-confidence is harming you and prevents you from succeeding in life. Developing your confidence requires taking practical steps, in addition to changing your beliefs or practicing positive thinking.

Each section is divided into easy to read chapters that contain information, insight, case studies, inspiration, and strategies that guarantee a rapid transformation in your life.

Besides discussing tips that will help you to grow your self-confidence, it further discusses the various ways for you to become a mentally stronger man. This book is packed with both theoretical and practical techniques for developing your own male self-confidence.

This book can be used as a guide from which you can select techniques that best fit you. This means you can develop your self-worth without even reading the entire book. Each part of the book is summed up with concise chapters that will help you go straight to the specific issues that you are lacking and that you wish to develop or strengthen.

Investing in developing your self-confidence is like investing in your whole life, and buying this book is the first step. I'm glad you have chosen to invest in yourself. Read this book at a pace that will allow you to absorb as much content as possible. Let the fantastic journey begin!

# PART 1: Self-Esteem

# Self-Esteem and Why You Need It

In this chapter, we will unravel what self-esteem is, its causes, how to overcome low-self-esteem, and explain why self-respect is important in your life, with particular emphasis on men.

Everyone in the world has self-esteem, men and women, teens and adolescents. Each has a way that they look at themselves. For example, happy people tend to have high self-esteem. On the other hand, people facing problems or stress will likely have low self-esteem. Additionally, some people exhibit excessive self-esteem that impedes their relationships with others. You are in one or more of these categories—recognizing which ones is the first step to fixing your self-esteem problems.

Self-esteem is defined as how you value yourself; it is how you perceive your value to the world and others around you. In psychology, self-esteem is defined as a sense of self-worth and personal value. Self-worth defines your competence in managing what life throws your way and it defines what it takes to feel worthy of happiness.

There is a thin line between self-esteem and self-acceptance. Self-esteem can be looked at as being internal, while self-acceptance is more about the perception outside of yourself. Self-esteem can be developed from any number of sources, including:

- Your self-appraisal.
- Family or parental support and approval.
- Acceptance by friends, colleagues, and teachers.
- How you handle challenges that come your way.

If you have positive self-esteem, you have mastered your self-acceptance, and you feel worthwhile because you feel you are contributing positively to the world. Lasting and robust self-esteem is usually based on your inherent qualities and unique characteristics.

## Why You Need Self-Esteem

Developing healthy self-esteem or self-worth will help you in many ways, including:

- When a loss or defeat happens, you will bounce back quicker and will be motivated to start anew faster.
- You will understand that falling down is inevitable, and that getting back on your feet is more important.
- It helps develop your ego, which will help you get a job, find a relationship, or pick yourself up after a failure.
- Positive self-esteem helps you to heal faster. It gives you the motivation to fight on and positively face the challenges that life throws at you.
- Positive self-esteem is the foundation of your wellness.
- Your happiness, psychological resilience, and impetus to live a productive and healthy life is dependent on your self-esteem.

Self-esteem is the belief that you are as worthwhile as anyone else. You should not confuse self-esteem with overconfidence, which can be a cause of failure in life.

In a nutshell, believing in yourself is the key to having happiness and success in your life. Self-esteem is more about how you feel about yourself as a person. Like many men, you may base your self-worth on external factors like the amount of money you make, what you own, your looks, or the number of friends you have. Unfortunately, these external factors often change, and this is bound to affect your self-esteem.

The exercises in this book will help you to grasp self-esteem from the inside, feeling competent and confident in how you handle life's challenges. It is the confidence in knowing that you can accomplish your goals and that you are contented with who you are.

## Consequences of Low Self-Esteem

Conversely, low self-esteem will often lead to depression, anxiety, anger issues, personal pain, and other distressing psychological problems.

- Low self-esteem will lead you to exhibit little or no regard for yourself; you will not respect or admire yourself.
- You will show a lack of confidence in yourself and will, in turn, belittle yourself with self-limiting thoughts.

Identifying the negative effects of low self-esteem in your life is the first step in realizing that you need to make changes in your life. If you feel you have a low sense of self-worth, it is important to recognize the bad habits that prevent you from achieving your personal goals.

If you have low self-worth, you will feel like nothing matters. You will feel like you are alone, even when you are with friends. Low self-esteem will make you feel disconnected from others. It makes you think that people are taking advantage of you and that they don't see you as an important person. This often leads to withdrawal, since you will be exhausted from trying to make people appreciate you, and hence you will end up giving up on life itself. If it is not handled in time, you may reach a point where you will see no reason for waking up in the morning, because you feel no one appreciates what you do and that they don't even care.

# Assessing Your Self-Esteem

When you need medication, you must present the drug store with a prescription before they give it to you. With self-esteem, you must be able to assess your current situation. In this test, you will be required to take a pen and paper and follow the instructions.

This exercise will help you understand what is lacking in your life, making it easier to find the tips in this book that will help you.

**Self-Esteem Test 1**

Write down the answers to these questions on a piece of paper:

1. What are the situations that cause you to feel inferior or to have a low sense of self-worth? Is it when you receive criticism? When you don't feel loved or when you are rejected? Describe the situations in detail.

2. What negative thoughts do you have? Do you often feel sad? Or inferior, or jealous? Describe here all the negative emotions that affect your self-esteem and confidence.

3. When you have a negative mindset, how do you handle that situation? Do you address yourself harshly or with self-respect? List some of the negative thoughts that affect you.

4. What is the consequence of low self-esteem? How does it affect your relationships?

5. Think of someone who you consider honorable and worthwhile. Who is this person? What makes you find him or her worthy? Describe the person in detail.

6. Do you have too much confidence? If yes, how does that differ from arrogance?

This exercise will help you to identify your self-esteem status. You will learn what affects your self-esteem; it's only when you can identify this that you can start to fix it.

Self-esteem enables you to appreciate yourself. Negative thoughts and beliefs will prevent you from reaching your potential. Cognitive therapy (CT) has been used in psychology to help men recognize and change these negative thoughts. Cognitive therapy is a well-researched methodology and is the primary treatment for depression.

Several factors can influence your thinking. For instance, the situations you experience in life can change how you think. If, for example, you have been abused sexually or repeatedly, you may think you have been treated as an object and may choose to be one. Your social environment, composed of media, friends, and family, can affect the way you think about things and the way you learn.

Although external events can influence the way you think, cognitive therapy assumes that you are individually responsible for the thoughts that you choose. You can't control how others treat or perceive you, but you can control how you think and what you think.

From the discussion above, you can see that self-esteem is a very elusive concept. You must decide what is important in your life and the steps or actions you need to take to achieve self-worth.

## Determining Your Self-Worth and Personality

Do you ever ask yourself, "Who am I?" Studies have suggested that your true self-esteem is based on who you are when no one is looking at you. And the only person who can answer that question is you. True self-worth is personal, in-depth, and complicated. Psychologists have suggested that you may have multiple selves, but, more often than not, you will choose one of those selves and focus on that.

People outside may look at you as a very bright, young, and happy man. Look at yourself and ask yourself if this is an accurate depiction of who you are. The public may have the wrong perception of who you are. This is a perception that you have created by how you package yourself up and present yourself to the outside world. Internally, your private self may differ significantly from your public self. You may pretend to be something that you are not just to fit in, or at least to avoid standing out.

If you have high self-esteem, you will find a way to blend your public and private self to create a close partnership; in this way, the two can complement each other to enhance your self-worth.

In the next test, I will use the self-esteem question to determine your personality. Establish whether you have a competency-driven personality or desirability-driven personality. Or if you have the characteristics of both types. Take out a pen and paper and honestly write down the answers to the questions below:

(Indicate whether it's: "True," "False," or you are "Undecided.")

7. You feel good when you get tasks done.

8. Your self-esteem increases when you get paid well for the work you do.

9. When your personal life conflicts with your professional obligations, you usually prioritize your professional responsibilities.

10. You don't compromise on everything in your life.

11. Even though you appreciate being told that you are loved, you prefer to be considered competent at what you do.

12. When something goes wrong, your first thought is how you might have messed things up.

13. You don't cancel an income-generating task for social engagements.

14. You don't take succeeding in love lightly and always work hard to excel at what you do.

15. You usually define yourself by what you do and not by how much your friends and family like you.

16. You can comfortably achieve things on your own, including luxuries like traveling and pursuing other interests.

17. You can't handle being competitive when faced with dire situations.

18. Even though you appreciate being told that you are a good guy, you prefer to be considered smart.

# Your Self-Esteem Analysis

After answering the 12 questions above, add up your "True" responses, followed by your "False" responses, and lastly, the "Undecided" responses. Write the scores on the piece of paper.

If you happened to answer "True" more than "False":

✔ It means that you base how you feel about yourself on how competent you are.

✔ You define yourself by the tasks you handle, and you care more about being capable of handling these tasks than being independent.

If you happened to answer more questions with "False" than the other two options:

✔ It means you base your feelings about yourself on your desirability.

✔ You are not concerned at all with what you do.

✔ You are keen on being liked and being seen as the right person for handling tasks.

If you have a lot of "Undecided" responses:

✔ It means you are high on both competency and desirability.

✔ You prefer being competent and liked at the same time.

✔ You are likely to be stressed, since both performance and interpersonal issues will cause you to doubt yourself.

Therefore, this test shows that self-esteem is a combination of self-confidence and self-respect. Your need for self-esteem is your need to know that the choices that you make are appropriate to your life and well-being. Since you must select your goals and actions, your sense of efficacy and security requires the belief that you are right in your method of choosing and making decisions. Self-confidence, on the other hand, is how reliant you are on your mind as a cognitive tool. It doesn't mean that you cannot make mistakes; it is instead the belief that you can think and judge correctly.

# Overcoming Insecurities and Self-Doubt

Self-doubt is a feeling that you have about your own abilities or actions. This means that self-doubt is not just about your present feelings, but it correlates with your past. This may cause you to say, "I have never been good at doing this and that, so why should I bother trying today?"

Self-doubt is a critical aspect of life, but when you have it in excess, it will drastically affect your confidence and will interfere with your ability to set and work toward your key objectives. Self-doubt will affect all aspects of your life, from your job to your leisure time and home activities, to relationships. Personal insecurities constrain affirmative action and cause distress, misery, and avoidance.

Coupled with fear—especially the fear of failure—self-doubt has the same effect that you might get when you try something new; for example, going on a first date, learning to swim, sky diving, or even skiing.

Self-doubt can make you become your own worst enemy. Being insecure will entirely crush your confidence. Men rarely attribute inadequacy to self-doubt, but your mood, action, arousal, and motivation are all directly affected by your sense of security. A financially insecure man will exhibit low self-esteem and a lack of confidence.

Doubt may cause you to underachieve and work below your real potential. Insecurities will make you feel that you are not prepared or skilled enough to handle a particular task—when, in the real sense, you are well equipped to handle the challenges before you.

This section will help you to recognize doubt and understand how it shapes your perspective of the world and, consequently, your feelings and responses.

## Causes of Self-Doubt

There are many events that may occur in your life that will lead you to doubt yourself or your capabilities. But the most prevalent causes of self-doubt or insecurities include:

- People looking down on you – this often happens when your friends or family ignore you or undermine your contribution in the activities that you think they should have consulted you on. Sometimes friends will give up on you; they may say that you are not good enough for the task at hand.
- Under-achievement – this occurs when you perform below the required standards. It may lead you to doubt your ability to accomplish critical tasks.
- Historical failures – past failures will make you fear certain activities that you believe you will fail at just because you did not succeed in the past.
- Unaccomplished objectives – you may fail to achieve your goals; discouraged because of fear, or if you have failed in the past and think that you should not try again.

# Effects of Self-Doubt

Self-doubt will negatively affect your performance and, at the same time, limit you from attaining your set objectives. Self-doubt will lead to:

- Little or no drive to achieve your goals.
- It will limit your success in life. Succeeding in life requires confidence and the belief that you can handle the challenges presented to you at any time.
- Self-doubt will lead you to have little or no sense of fulfillment. To lead a fulfilling life, you need confidence in yourself and the satisfaction that your friends and relatives have confidence in your abilities.

As highlighted in the above discussion, insecurities and self-doubts constitute a significant concern, and they inhibit your ability to face challenges in life and to reach your peak performance. Thus, it is necessary to find effective ways of overcoming self-doubt. Now it begs the question, how should you overcome self-doubt and insecurities?

# Six Effective Remedies for Overcoming Self-Doubt

To conquer self-doubt, you should develop habits that will push you to see the big picture and that you are in control of your life. There are several ways to overcome self-doubt, and you will find below a discussion of six effective means of curing self-doubt:

1. **Acknowledge your capabilities**. You are not supposed to always play it safe and chase the low hanging fruits. You should push yourself to achieve more than you think you can handle. From childhood, you are trained to follow specific norms and to believe realistically. But this approach can, at the same time, be limiting; it will discourage you from tackling new challenges.

**2. Disregard negative voices within you.** The adage "hear no evil" makes sense here. When you close your ears to negative voices, you will achieve more and exceed expectations. Negative views will affect your motivation to achieve your goals. Society may send negative signals to you. For example, it can sway you to quit pursuing a particular goal. These negative voices should "fall on deaf ears" for you to achieve your objectives without limiting thoughts. You should stand up for what you think is right. Stick by your goals and desires. If you do this, you are more likely to retire a happy man because you will not regret what you have not done in the past. You will have little or no "unfinished business."

**3. Have your support group.** Take the example of Nick Vujicic. Vujicic was born without arms and legs and is considered a warrior when it comes to confidence and self-doubt. He has beaten all odds by doing just about everything—from swimming, to cooking and dancing, among others. Nick Vujicic does everything an average human being does. He currently motivates people through his organization called "Life Without Limbs."

Nick Vujicic motivates fellow men and women who are born with the same condition. To achieve all these things, he has received great help and assistance from his support group. These are the people who encourage and help him to soldier on in life. They can be friends, family, sponsors, organizations, and societies that believe that his cause to transform people is worthy. Nick Vujicic's parents never gave up on him. His parents encouraged him to try everything, because they thought that he would never know what he can and cannot do if he doesn't try it out.

With that positive affirmation and support from his parents, Vujicic learned how to fish, swim, snowboard, bath, and live independently. Vujicic was determined not to be a burden to anybody, even his wife, Kanae. Vujicic's wife, Kanae, gives excellent support to him through thick and thin. They now have a lovely family together.

Men often need a support group to uplift their spirits every day. These are the people that care about you, and they will make you feel better when things go south. The advice and counsel of such people matters a lot in your decisions and, as a result, directly affects your confidence and self-esteem.

**4. Be modest and always willing to learn.** Ego can cause you to either underachieve or over-achieve. It is the ego that keeps you in check. As Newton's third law of motion states: for every action, there is always an equal and opposite reaction. Therefore, an overinflated ego may seem fine at first. You may have fun showing off, bragging, and looking down upon your peers. But when situations change and you fail in one thing or the other, the experience will be very traumatizing. You will crash and may take longer to recover.

It is because of this that you are encouraged to have humility of the highest order. Being humble is closely related to self-doubt. Humility is a trait that is welcomed by many people. It is the trait that will help you to calmly make decisions during the highs and lows of life. You will only succeed in life if you put your overall objectives above the desire to be recognized.

Besides, you should have a thirst for knowledge. You should be willing to learn new things. As a result, you will end up doing many things, and these successes will help grow your self-confidence. At any time in this life, provided you are healthy, there will be more to learn and even much more to improve.

**5. Strive to beat your record daily.** If you are successful, you will always strive to beat your previous achievements, as opposed to beating other people. It is detrimental to compare yourself to other people. In life, our destinies and efforts vary greatly. You have your own time to succeed, your own goals, and your own view of life.

Some people will be lucky. Luck is a huge factor that is often underestimated by many. But humans fail in many ways. You may meet the wrong person or partner in life, leading them with you on the path to failure. The road to success is unique for every human being. You cannot copy another person's success and make it yours. It doesn't work that way.

It is crucial to evaluate your capabilities and set practical goals for yourself. This is because, if you strive to become the next Bill Gates, your journey will be marred with self-doubt because your goal is not realistic, and you will eventually be disappointed.

**6. Always work hard.** The reality of life is that not everybody will be talented enough or will have the ability to succeed in a specific field. But once you accept this about yourself, you can then have confidence, patience, and perseverance to assist you in your achievements.

Working hard entails putting in some more effort continuously with the end goal in mind. By so doing, you will be insulating yourself from self-doubt because you will always have the desire to keep trying constantly. Just like Thomas Edison once said, we should not call it a failure, but instead, it's just 10,000 ways that won't work. Keep working hard, and remember that the shortcomings in the world outweigh the successes. Only if you have the willpower to move past your failures will you be successful. You should not allow room in your mind for self-doubt. Always be determined to climb, without letting negative voices or other people bring you down.

# Self-Doubt Test

When you are about to face a challenge in life, and you think your self-doubt and insecurities may pull you down, it is important to take a self-doubt test that will help you to identify the areas where you should be vigilant. You will need a pen and paper to do this test. This is a simple "Yes" or "No" test that will help you discover what is limiting your capabilities. Tick either "Yes" or "No":

Imagine you were offered a job at your dream company. You have been struggling for years to get this chance, and now it has presented itself. Take this test on what you imagine is the day of the interview or appointment. You can also take this test before a real job interview, or new job.

- Do you have the necessary skills to do this job?
  _ Yes _ No
- Did your previous employment prepare you for this new job?
  _ Yes _ No
- You grasp new concepts fast.
  _ Yes _ No
- You always ask questions when you need help.
  _ Yes _ No
- When faced with a challenge, you always soldier through.
  _ Yes _ No
- You are calm even in tense situations.
  _ Yes _ No
- You can handle this job.
  _ Yes _ No

# Test Analysis

How many questions did you answer "Yes" to above? If your answer to at least five questions was "Yes," then you are in the best state of mind to face the job. It means you are capable of handling the job responsibilities. Thus, you should not doubt your capability to handle the task at hand. Go with a straight mind that you will shine at the job.

If you answered "Yes" to less than five questions, then it means you have some self-doubt. It means you doubt your ability to handle the tasks that the job requires you to handle. Self-doubt usually leads you to ask yourself unrealistic questions and may hinder you from achieving what you are skilled to achieve. Here, you should try re-affirming yourself, because if this is your area of expertise, you must be able to handle the situation at hand.

From the above test, we can see that there is a thin line between realistic concerns and self-doubt. It means you may stress yourself and look down on yourself—simply because you doubt yourself. Identifying this self-doubt is the first step in your journey to success.

# Body Image: How Important Is It?

What do you think about your body image? Do you like it? Would you wish it was in some way different? If so, then you aren't alone: many people don't like the way their body is structured.

Most likely, you have looked at yourself in the mirror and thought that you look fat, or too thin. You have emphasized the flaws on your face, thinking the nose is too large, lips are too small or too big, and so on. These negative affirmations put yourself down. Men always look at their shoulders and think they are not broad enough, or that their stomach is bulging, or they believe that they are not manly enough. Men are just as concerned about looks as women are. Body image is something that every human being has to contend with.

Your body image is your natural look. It comprises of how you look, weigh, whether you are tall, short, et cetera. Your self-worth will affect the way you see your own body and how you deal with body image matters. When you have low self-esteem, it means you look at your body in a negative light. When you look at yourself in the mirror every day, all you see are flaws, and you will often point out everything you think is wrong with your body.

This may lead you to ignore things that you can do to make yourself look better, like eating healthy, exercising regularly, and dressing up. Low self-worth can make you hate your body, and you may end up not looking at yourself in the mirror.

Looking down on yourself and how your body looks like may lead you to destructive habits like starving yourself, anorexia, binge eating, and sometimes bulimia. Such practices can be life-threatening if not treated in time. And as you get older, the changes in your body become even more challenging.

From the explanation above, you will notice that body image has a lot to do with how you relate to your body. It is your relationship with your body, how you think about yourself, feel about yourself, and your view of what good looking is. In this section, we will explore how you relate to your body and how important this is to your self-worth. It is possible to look at yourself in a positive light and to love your body image.

Your body image is how you see yourself in your mind. As a man, you may often underestimate your body size and masculinity. If you are dissatisfied with your body image, it will make you unhappy for your entire life. Changing your body image can be a frustrating and disappointing endeavor.

Remember, feeling good about how you look has a lot to do with things other than just your weight and body shape. Men are always concerned about their looks, although there is the perception that women are more vocal about their looks and invest a significant amount of time and money in enhancing their looks at any given time. This book will look at body image in a broader sense. The journey toward accepting how you look can be challenging. But this section will explore the strategies necessary to improve your self-confidence by first accepting your body image, how you look, and how you wish others to perceive you.

## Feeling Good About Your Looks

Let's use an example of "Paul"—for this, you are Paul. You are a smart and attractive lawyer. You have achieved a lot in your life and your workmates like you. But you are always alone at home when it comes to attending parties and movie nights. When asked, you may say that you have been too busy to socialize lately. But the truth of the matter remains that you are afraid to meet new people; and worse still, you are scared of meeting and talking to ladies.

You have a receding hairline that makes you think that no one will like you that way. You usually avoid asking ladies out unless pushed by friends. Even when you are on a date, you do not concentrate on the conversation because you are always thinking that the lady is looking at your hair. You look at the receding hairline as balding, a unique feature that your peers don't have. Your self-doubt creeps into your job, and you start missing appointments with colleagues.

With this example, we see body image as an inner personal view of your outer body. It is how you perceive your own body and your overall appearance. How you appear for real has little relation to your sense of attractiveness. When a man is handsome, this doesn't guarantee the right body image. You can be beautiful but still be dissatisfied with your looks. You can be told several times that you look good, but you see yourself in an entirely different light.

**Why Do You Look at Yourself Differently?**

Body image has a lot to do with how you see yourself. A poor body image will focus on the parts of the body that you hate, and forget the ones that you find attractive. Consequently, you may have a distorted view of yourself. You may be preoccupied and worry about your skin tone, and never pay any attention to your own attractive smile, a feature that people see quickly the first time you meet.

Your body image will affect how you:
1. Think;
2. Feel; and
3. Act.

A negative body image will make you feel dissatisfied about yourself, and you will end up wasting time being preoccupied with yourself. It can make you feel inadequate and frustrated. On the contrary, the right body image makes you more self-confident, increases your self-esteem, and you end up liking yourself more.

An adverse body image will make you beat yourself up for your small flaws. It makes you monitor your environment keenly for clues that relate to your appearance. This makes you very sensitive when people are around you, and more so when someone comments on your looks. This will cause you to be very insecure, anxious in social setups, and you will avoid some things, since they make you feel uncomfortable. It makes you feel less masculine, which will, in turn, reduce your sexual pleasure, and that can lead to also hurting your self-confidence.

A negative body image makes you feel that you are a less desirable person, and will make you feel discouraged about your future. This may sometimes even cause you to stay the whole day indoors, since you don't want people to look at you. It may cause you to compare yourself with people that you consider more attractive and thus will make you spend a lot of time and effort trying to improve your looks. This habit, feeling, and behavior will cause you to fail or feel inferior. The more you feel dissatisfied with your looks, the longer that feeling will stay, and thus the more you are likely to suffer as a result.

To handle a negative body image, consider that you are not alone in this world. Yes, you are uniquely made, but it doesn't mean no other people are sharing your peculiar features. Many people are dissatisfied with how they look. This often increases at some stage in life like puberty and teenage age or middle age. At this stage, you may become sensitive to how your hair, skin, and even clothing looks.

**What Is a Natural Look?**

If you are concerned about how you look, you are better off trying to eliminate some concern about normality and instead examine how the same concerns are impacting your own life. Being discontented with your appearance should be handled carefully, as it can end up severely affecting you. Thinking about looks can affect your whole day, leaving you attached to the mirror and concerned that you don't look right.

The critical factor here is how preoccupied you are with how you look and how it is affecting your life. There is a thin line between having a healthy and unhealthy outlook, especially in a society that is full of people who are not satisfied with how they look.

It's tough to decide whether distress and impairment as a result of doubts about appearance should be considered normal, or should be categorized as a psychiatric sickness. Severe worries about looks is a sign of some mental disorders too. Therefore, Body Dysmorphic Disorder (BDD) needs to be diagnosed by a specialist who comprehends the differences. If you have anorexia nervosa, for instance, you are always concerned about how you look, but anorexia is often associated with harshly disturbed eating habits, and the preoccupation with appearance focuses entirely on weight.

Symptoms of BDD often resemble other disorders, which can easily cause misdiagnosis and the wrong treatment to be delivered.

BDD usually begins during adolescence. It becomes chronic, even lasting longer without improvement. BDD is more prevalent in men as compared to women.

## How Do You Know You Have BDD?

It is crucial to have an idea of how severe your issue is before you address it. Therefore, the test below may give you clues as to whether you have BDD or not. This diagnosis can only be made by a qualified professional, however. This book will only offer you guidance on how to identify the signs and symptoms of BDD.

In case you answer "Yes" to all of the questions, your problem is not related to bad eating habits; instead, you may be suffering from BDD. When your BDD is extremely distressing or impairing, you should visit a clinician. Similarly, if you doubt your ability to use self-help, consider engaging a qualified psychiatrist with experience in handling BDD. This is a sensitive disorder and often mishandled by people who don't have a clear idea of how it should be treated.

**Signs of BDD**

Answer the following questions honestly. These questions will give clues as to whether you are affected by BDD or not.

**1.** Do you hate the way you look?

**2.** Do you think about how you look for more than three hours daily?

**3.** Do you consider your worries about your looks as being excessive, or have people told you that you look beautiful or handsome and that you worry too much about how you look?

**4.** Do you involve yourself in activities with the intention of hiding, or fixing your looks? For instance, looking at the mirror, comparing yourself with other people, and excessive grooming behaviors.

**5.** Do you avoid places, people, or activities just because of your looks? For instance, do you keep out of bright lights or avoid mirrors, dates, or huge parties?

**6.** Do your looks-related thoughts or habits make you anxious, sad, or ashamed of yourself?

**7.** Do you have difficulties with your work, school, neighbors, family, or friends because of your concerns about your looks?

**Depression as a Sign of BDD**

Everyone feels down sometimes, that is normal. But in case your depression lasts longer and causes distress, you may have a problem that needs urgent action. If you suspect that you are suffering from depression, take a look at these symptoms:

- Always feeling down, unhappy, and short-tempered: for many weeks, sometimes longer.
- Reduced desire to engage in your hobbies and leisure activities.
- Feeling tired and have low energy, in spite of lack of activity.
- Increased or reduced appetite, with noteworthy weight gain or loss.
- Trouble sleeping, waking up too early in the morning or sleeping more than usual.
- Feeling slowed down, restless or fidgety, diminished ability to make decisions or difficulty concentrating.
- Feeling worthless, guilty, or hopeless.
- Excessive thoughts of suicide or death.

Over 75% of people with BDD show signs of depression. Therefore, if you have been diagnosed with BDD or you think you have it, and you are also experiencing some of the above symptoms, seek the help of a professional.

# Even Men Need Self-Love!

It has often been misinterpreted that only women should have an excessive love for themselves. This is the wrong assumption because men equally should love themselves. Men are known to be selfless and often do not care much about themselves. But recently, this is changing, and more and more men are developing self-love.

Loving yourself is a challenge that emanates from your personal feelings of inadequacy. More and more men should be challenged to love themselves as a way of empowering them to confront the negative thoughts that they often harbor. Once the negative thoughts have been handled, you will usually start shifting to a positive experience with your entire mind and body.

When you have a limiting belief or negative attitude toward yourself, you will always be weighed down by your negativity. Once you treat yourself with love, respect, and self-care, you will genuinely grow and shine, treating others the same.

We have all learned that loving other people is a good thing, and we forget to love ourselves, although loving oneself has never been considered as a big issue. But why is this?

It may be an assumption that you automatically love yourself. Hence the only love you are supposed to work on is your love for others. By so doing, the things that affect individuals like stress and depression will not be addressed in time.

Many men don't know how to practice self-love. And you may even offensively and inappropriately equate self-love to being "gay" or "a sissy." But self-love is as important to men as it is for women. To develop self-love, you should form habits; positive habits that will boost your self-worth. In this section, we will discuss the habits that you should develop to practice self-love. There are many ways to practice self-love for men, but we will focus on the thirteen most important habits.

## Thirteen Habits to Practice in Order to Develop Self-Love

### 1. Take a picture of yourself and keep it in your phone.

Men often consider taking "selfies" as being feminine. To increase your self-worth, it is essential to look at yourself repeatedly and affirm yourself. There is a lot of pressure in the world to look good. How many pictures do you take of yourself and then delete before you post what you consider the perfect shot to social media?

You should believe that you always look good, and affirm yourself irrespective of what you consider as a flaw. Therefore, take a photo of yourself, no matter how rugged you look, look at it, and let it stay strategically on your phone. If you like it so much, go ahead and share it on social media of your choice. This action will increase your self-love tenfold.

You can also do a mini photoshoot with a friend or family member. This will let the model in you out. Be stupid and sultry sometimes. Let yourself be free and be the star for a moment, realize that you can express yourself in any way you wish in this world.

### 2. Look at yourself in the mirror and appreciate what you like about yourself.

This workout can be challenging to achieve because your instinct will be to first pick the negatives about yourself. You need to push that negative voice away, even if it's only briefly. Practice doing this daily to allow positive thoughts to prevail; try positive affirmations and saying things like: "My nose looks great." Try to find the positives, and you'll eventually have a different perspective on everything.

### 3. Make a list of what you love in others.

If you work hard and make other people happy, you will automatically be loved back by society, family, and friends. This will increase your self-worth and, in turn, make you love yourself more and more. Such achievement is bound to boost your self-confidence and feelings of self-worth. When other people appreciate what you do for them, you will feel that you are worthy of being in the world and that you are contributing to a worthy cause. Think about the attributes you love in the people around you, and celebrate those, making them feel valued and appreciated.

When you practice doing this often, you will be a people magnet, and the entire community will appreciate you and will wish to hang around you or copy what you are doing. Thus, when you love yourself, others will automatically understand it and love you back even more. Regularly practicing this will help you to figure out the kind of person that you would like to be.

### 4. Read a book or a poem.

Reading is an intimate connection to the thoughts, likes, and subjects that the author loves. When you practice reading self-help books regularly, it will help to boost your self-worth. Poetry has the power to make people feel special. Love poems can be soothing or sad. Sometimes, poems will be flowery and very beautiful, and at times they will be straight to the point. Poems do open people up to love. Reading a poem or a romantic book is equivalent to falling in love and being in the author's world, and reading can give you new perspectives on life and help you to "step into someone else's shoes," which can develop compassion for yourself and others.

**5. Love yourself – hug yourself and tell yourself that you love yourself.**

When you love yourself, other people will love you. The world will resonate around you in the frequency that you set yourself. If you are positive about yourself and your peers, family, and friends, the world will respond with positivity too. Hugging yourself may seem silly. But that little moment will increase your self-worth tenfold. Never be afraid of showing yourself affection. When you love yourself, you will remember that you should also treat others the way you would treat yourself. That is with honesty and care. When you dearly love yourself, you open windows for yourself to love others.

**6. Keep a diary of your recent achievements.**

Here, you should develop the habit of recording or documenting your accomplishments. For example, take a pen and paper and write what you accomplished in the last day, followed by week, then the entire previous month. Record your achievements on the paper. Sometimes this can motivate you, but sometimes it may leave you feeling worthless, especially if you underachieved in the past. When you do this, you will be able to organize your pending tasks and know how far behind schedule you may have been. The bottom line is, when you diarize events, it helps you to plan better for the future.

**7. Run away from negativity.**

Negative thoughts are brought about by what we regularly feed our minds. If you continuously feed your brain with limiting beliefs, it will become part of you, and it will manifest in your poor performance and reduced self-confidence, since your ego will already have been punctured. Harmful gadgets and pieces of technology should also be avoided to nurture positive thinking. You should unfollow and exit blogs and social media sites that don't add value to your life. You should spend your time on important things. Join social media sites and websites that applaud their members and uplift them rather than weighing them down.

### 8. Declutter your life.

Go through your wardrobe and give away everything that you don't require. By so doing, your self-worth will increase. This is because you will develop an inner feeling of having achieved something, like helping a needy person. You may have developed the habit of keeping stuff in your house, things that you rarely use. This is like carrying a dead weight that is not necessary, a burden that can be offloaded, and you will still function well. All this means is that you should reduce the dead weight and leave only clothes that fit you perfectly and are still in good condition.

### 9. Surround yourself with positive people.

This can be a challenge that you are likely to find difficult. It is very sensitive, and the chances are that someone's feelings will be hurt in the process. And you are not an exception, since the injured feelings can be yours. Ultimately, though, this will have a significant positive impact on your life. It is quite easy to stick around with friends who pull you down, brush you off, and leave your ego hurt in the process. This is not easy for your mental well-being or self-image. You should surround yourself with people who will raise you and you can ascend to new heights together.

Of course, this is easier said than done. It's challenging to end friendships, mainly when they date back. It is essential to talk to the friends to give them a chance to understand their behavior and to change, before cutting them off. You can even go up a notch and write a letter if you are uncomfortable talking to them face to face. Ensure they know how their behavior or lifestyle derails you. People often don't understand that their comments can be hurting or wrecking you. If they try changing, you will have strengthened your friendship in turn. On the other hand, if they refuse to change for the better, you will consider yourself to have achieved what you set out to, since you spoke your mind from the outset and now you can let go of the negative friendship.

### 10. Learn something new every day.

In the past, you were young, and the entire world looked new. You can re-live the past by harnessing thoughts that build your brain. Every so often, you should allow yourself to read either a book, blog, periodical, journal, or article. You should spend some time learning something new from these books or physically as well. Try something out of your zone, like designing a website, or playing golf. Try learning how to play the guitar gradually from the basic chords to complicated notes.

### 11. Treat yourself.

You should consider treating yourself by taking yourself out for dinner and walks. Treat yourself to your favorite movie. You can choose a film from your childhood and watch it to enjoy it. Let yourself relax for a while and revisit the favorite parts of your past. From this, you can derive lessons that you will use in your future endeavors.

### 12. Practice self-talk.

Weird as it may seem, self-talk is critical when you wish to address issues about yourself. You need to interrogate yourself seriously. As discussed under body image in the previous section, you may be having problems with how a specific part of your body looks. Have a talk with this part of the body and about it at the same time. Self-talk should always be positive. Talk to yourself now and then, and by so doing, the negative thoughts will be blocked from your mind.

### 13. Practice forgiving yourself.

Everybody makes mistakes. But you still like blaming yourself over small errors that you have committed. Think of the transformation that you wish to witness in the long run. Then forgive yourself. Appreciate what has occurred but remind yourself that those are bygones and deal with the emerging consequences.

Significant growth in yourself will be achieved when you forgive yourself. It is easy to keep asking yourself the question "What if?" which will make you stagnate. You cannot move forward in that manner. Forgiving yourself means that you appreciate yourself as a human and that you accept you are imperfect and flawed as all humans are.

The above thirteen habits are just a few of the practices that, if done repeatedly, will enable you to love yourself.

# Thirteen Self-Esteem Habits to Practice Daily

This section will give you thirteen simple, easy to implement, habits that will uplift you and increase your positive self-esteem. Committing to practicing these habits will wisely utilize your time and, in turn, will improve your life.

It doesn't take long to develop your self-esteem. There are myriad things that you can do to improve your self-worth and enhance your life. The thirteen habits detailed below have been carefully selected among many. The practices are short and to the point:

**1. Choose and become proficient at something you love.**

Establish a skill doing something that you love. It will require hard work and dedication to achieve this, but at the end of it, it will be worth the effort you put into it. To achieve this, you must be willing to stick to it and be determined to succeed.

To enjoy life, you must focus your potential on what you do well, rather than on your limitations. You must maximize your innate aptitudes and abilities. Every man has a weakness, and it will take courage for you to admit your shortcomings. But it is soothing to realize that you have your strengths and acknowledge that you have talents and personal qualities that others don't have.

There are different approaches to achieving this; you can either read books on the subject, talk to people in the field of your interest, or search the web and electronic media for information about the topic that interests you.

As the saying goes, "Practice makes perfect." To become proficient in a skill faster, you must practice it more often. While at it regularly, you will keep improving continuously to get better at that skill. As your competency in doing the activity grows, it will be a source of satisfaction and accomplishment for you.

The world is full of unsuccessful but talented men, but they lack confidence and persistence. You may feel, like them, that no matter how proficient you are at something, someone elsewhere is better than you. You shouldn't be one of them.

### 2. Research online, read books and articles that uplift you.

If you look down upon yourself, you can improve your self-worth by reading materials that help you look on the bright side of your life. You can adjust your life by taking control of what you consume online and from books.

Watching TV shows, movies, and commercials will reduce your self-worth and make you feel like you are not good enough. Your self-esteem may decrease if that is what consumes much of your time.

You should read material that underscores self-improvement, motivation, and other ways to raise your mood.

### 3. Always review your day's activities.

At the close of the day, evaluating what went well during the day can help to develop your self-worth. Get into the habit of setting aside a few minutes to discuss the events of the day with yourself. The right way of approaching this is by closing your eyes and relaxing. With your eyes closed, try to go through the events of the day. Start with the morning, then midday, until you have evaluated the events of that evening. Evaluate the events that occurred, people you interacted with, and, most importantly, the decisions you made, including successes and failures of the day.

You should be thankful for all that went well during the day. To improve your self-worth, identify at least four things that you achieved successfully; always be grateful for the things that you did well during the day. After that, note the things that you could have done differently.

This simple exercise helps you to identify the good that happens in your life and shows you how you can improve it in the future.

### 4. Avoid behaviors that waste your time.

Discover your bad habits, and try to avoid them. Bad habits can include watching TV, playing games, excessive Internet, et cetera. These are time-wasting habits that add nothing to your sense of self-worth. In this case, you should either completely stop these habits or reduce the time allotted to them. Use those hours to do constructive, creative, and positive things.

To identify the habits that waste your time, ask yourself the following questions:

✔ What excites you most?

✔ What do you like doing, or what can you do without being forced to do it?

✔ What end results do you want to achieve?

### 5. List all your achievements.

When you feel you have a low opinion about yourself, consider listing all your accomplishments. This small exercise will transform your focus. To do this exercise:

✔ Get a pen and paper or use online systems. Set a time limit for the activity; this will help you to avoid spending a lot of time on the task.

✔ Jot down all your achievements—both when you were young and at present.

✔ The list should contain achievements of whichever magnitude: big or small.

✔ The list should include not only what you have done for yourself, but also what you have done for others.

Once you have made the list of achievements, read through them several times, affirming yourself for the achievements listed.

**6. Go out with friends.**

True friends will like you for who you are and will provide companionship based on that. Going out with friends will improve your bond with them. Going out includes going to watch movies or live music, shopping, the park, bowling, dinner, parties, the gymnasium, and sports events, et cetera.

**7. Teach others a skill that you have perfected.**

The mere fact that you can impart knowledge of a skill that you have developed to others will increase your self-confidence. When you teach others, you become a role model for them. Teaching will help you look at yourself positively as a change maker. Here, self-confidence is having the belief that you are capable of achieving something. It means you respect yourself and you believe that you have worth, irrespective of what you make out of it.

Helping students gain more insight into a specific skill will build your students' self-confidence and self-esteem too.

**8. Plan a fun-filled road trip.**

Planning a trip is usually for adventure and the accompanied excitement. The planning stage of the journey will give you a sense of belonging and worth. If you are allowed by your friends and family to plan for the trip, it will boost your self-worth, because you will look at yourself as a contributor to the activity.

The planning process will include some team activities like:

✔ Talking to your colleagues or friends and family who want to join in.

✔ Making and sharing a list of the fun activities that the places you have chosen to visit offer, for instance, beaches, museums, et cetera.

✔ Considering the weather patterns of the destination, and what to take for the journey.

### 9. Volunteering to support a cause.

Helping others for free will always make you feel good about yourself. Volunteering helps you get connected to your peers and have pride in the cause. At the same time, volunteering gives you a chance to give back to the community.

There are many benefits of volunteering that lead to increased feelings of self-worth; these include:

✔ Helping you to build your contacts and make new friends or connections. Such connections are necessary for positive self-esteem.

✔ Enabling you to practice and perfect your social skills.

✔ Feeling good that you are implementing something that important and worthy to others.

✔ Making those that you are assisting happy, and at the same time, you will be happy when everything goes as planned.

✔ Granting you the chance to try new things.

✔ Equipping you with new transferrable skills.

When you decide to volunteer to a cause(s), you shouldn't limit yourself to one organization. It is good to volunteer for many organizations; to embrace learning opportunities, and to establish whether you connect with staff.

### 10. Remember that your circumstances do not define you.

Negative thoughts will always lead to low self-worth. Never allow your circumstances to determine who you are. Remember that the situation you are in is temporary.

Try distancing yourself from situations that lead you nowhere. If you are dissatisfied with events that occurred in your past, you should understand that they don't determine who you are.

### 11. Read and write a review of your favorite book.

To top it off, you can take a selfie photo when you finish reading a book and post it to a group of like-minded readers. Doing this will improve your self-worth, since you will appreciate yourself for finishing the book. Then post a review of the book online, either on your blog or on social media. Books are amazing. Once you develop the habit of reading empowering books, your self-esteem will automatically increase.

### 12. List five things or more about yourself.

As discussed earlier, list the internal things that define you. Now, here we will consider the physical things that you can do to improve your self-esteem. There are several things you can do. Therefore, you should make a list of positive things that you can achieve with minimal effort. On those days that you can't seem to love yourself, get this list out and read it over and over again.

### 13. Put positive messages on sticky notes on your mirror.

The mirror is one spot in the house that, come what may, you will have to visit every day. It is important to surround the mirror and the entire house with positive messages. Looking at these messages every day will help to make them permanent in your mind. The sticky notes can have motivational quotes that will help trigger something in you every time you look at them.

The thirteen habits listed above are just a few among many that can boost your self-esteem. If practiced daily, religiously, and consistently, these habits will become an innate part of you. You will not even notice how you will be accomplishing them, as the processes will be so swift and effortless.

# PART 2: Self-Confidence

# Self-Esteem Vs. Self-Confidence

In part one, we explored a lot about self-esteem. In this section, we will compare self-esteem and confidence. There is a thin line between the two. Men will always wish to be confident and have high self-esteem. You may not say it aloud, but the desire is there within you.

Self-esteem and self-confidence are composite words. They are made of two parts: "self" and esteem, "self" and confidence. The first part of these words is significant.

Confidence can be viewed in three perspectives:

- As self-assuredness—here, the definition relates to your self-confidence as your ability to perform to a certain standard.
- Belief in other peoples' abilities—here, confidence emphasizes on how you would like others to behave in a trustworthy or competent manner.
- Keeping information secret or restricted to some people—here confidence is defined as hiding information from other people.

This means that confidence is not all about feeling good inside, although feeling good is a bonus.

Confidence comes with practice and how you familiarize yourself with what you do. Below are eight signs that indicate whether you are confident enough:

✔ You will be poised and well balanced.

✔ You are breathing effortlessly.

✔ You are moving toward your objectives in life smoothly and with a sense of purpose.

✔ You are proactive rather than reactive and defensive.

✔ You respond to situations and challenges rather than reacting to them.

✔ You are sure that you can deal with whatever life throws at you, even if it is out of your control.

✔ You can afford to laugh at yourself.

✔ You believe that everything will be fine in the end, however long it takes.

This section will help you to find your inner confidence and enable you to take the first step in your journey to success, however scary or hard it may seem at the moment.

## Ten Indicators of Confidence

Below are ten signs of a confident man. When you act with confidence, you are likely to have some of these ten qualities:

**1. Self-direction and value.** If you are a confident man, you will know what you want and where you are heading and what is important to you.

**2. Motivated.** Confidence leads to high motivation, and you will enjoy what you do. You may be so engaged in what you do that you cannot be distracted by anything.

**3. Exhibit emotional stability.** As a confident man, you are more likely to be calm and focused on how you approach people and challenges. You will be able to sense difficult emotions like anger and anxiety and will work with them instead of letting them overcome you.

**4. Think positive.** Confidence leads to a positive mindset. You can stay optimistic and always see the bright side of everything, including challenges and setbacks. You hold positive regard for yourself and others.

**5. Aware of yourself.** You know what you are good at, and what you can handle. You know how you look and sound to others. You acknowledge that you are a human being and that you are not perfect.

**6. Flexibility.** You adapt your behavior according to the situation at hand. You can see the bigger picture while at the same time being attentive to details. You always consider other people's views while making decisions.

**7. Eager to develop.** You enjoy stretching yourself. You treat every day as a learning experience instead of acting as if you are an expert with nothing new to learn.

**8. Healthy and energetic.** You are in touch with your body and respect it, and you have a sense that your energy is flowing freely. You can handle stressful situations without burning out.

**9. Willing to take risks.** You can take risks and act in the face of uncertainty. You will put yourself on the line even when you don't have the necessary skills and answers to the situation at hand.

**10. Has a sense of purpose.** You have a high sense of the coherence of different aspects of your life.

## Self-Confidence Test

The 20-point questionnaire below is derived from the confidence indicators above. To measure your confidence level, answer all the questions by indicating whether you agree or disagree with the statements in the five-point scale provided. You should take the test as many times as you like and keep track of the development.

Once you have taken the test, keep the results in a diary and do it again in four to six months, and note the development. Completing this test will help you to discover the aspects of your life that affect your confidence. Try to answer the questions accurately so that you can correctly evaluate your level of trust and prescribe the right remedy for what is lacking. Check where applicable.

| Statement | Strongly Agree | Agree | Neutral | Disagree | Strongly agree |
|---|---|---|---|---|---|
| You know what is important to you. | | | | | |
| You know what you need in life. | | | | | |
| You never hate yourself for failing. | | | | | |
| You can stay calm and think when things get difficult. | | | | | |
| All you do involves things you love doing. | | | | | |
| You often become fully engrossed in what you are doing. | | | | | |
| You are quite optimistic. | | | | | |
| You respect yourself and people around you. | | | | | |
| You know your strengths and weaknesses. | | | | | |
| You know what others consider to be your strengths. | | | | | |
| You consult others where necessary, before taking action. | | | | | |
| You are ok with looking at the big picture and intricate details in situations. | | | | | |

| | | | | | |
|---|---|---|---|---|---|
| You enjoy taking up new challenges. | | | | | |
| You love looking for new opportunities and learning and growing from them. | | | | | |
| You look after your body image. | | | | | |
| You handle stress well. | | | | | |
| You have a positive attitude toward taking risks. | | | | | |
| You regularly meditate. | | | | | |
| You have your set mission and purpose in life. | | | | | |
| You are self-motivated to handle new challenges. | | | | | |

After checking the appropriate square on each line of the questionnaire, award yourself five points for each check under the "Strongly agree" column, four points in the "Agree" column, three points for "Neutral," two points for "Disagree," and one point in the "Strongly disagree" column.

Add the points up and analyze the results. Use the rating scale below for advice based on your score. This activity will help you to know the areas of your life that require immediate attention and the sections of this book that you should skip to read immediately.

**Rating**

**Score: 80 – 100.** This means by all standards, you are a confident person. It means you have clear priorities and hopefully pursue the life you desire.

**Score: 60 – 80.** You are confident in many situations. Just a few areas in your life pull you down. You have a burning desire to improve your confidence and increase your self-worth. This book will help you on your journey to trusting yourself. Look at the next part of this book to improve on these aspects.

**Score: 40 - 60**. You have picked the right book. The tips and tricks in this book will help you to improve this score in a couple of months if followed religiously. You are just experiencing some uncertainty in your life at the moment, and you may be wondering whether you can do anything to address the situation. You need to allow yourself some time to work on the aspects that require immediate attention, and you will be happy with your progress in a few months.

**Score: 20 - 40**. You have very low self-confidence, but not to worry because it doesn't have to stay that way. The fact that you have taken the test has set you on the right path to building your confidence. Even if you have scored below par in this test, you can increase your self-confidence tenfold in the next 4-6 months by following the steps and principles outlined in this book. Read this book cover to cover, and you will find excellent advice that will put you on the right path to self-worth.

Once you have finished the exercise and read the advice based on your score, look at the score and note the parts that brought down your overall rating. Read chapters related to improving those specific areas of confidence. Do the exercise some months later, and you will notice progress in your evaluation. This book is full of advice and practical guidance to help you improve all the aspects that affect your self-worth.

Go over the content to identify the areas that will help you to boost your confidence quickly. The test above is simple but very powerful in monitoring the growth of your belief in yourself. The activity will also enable you to identify your strengths and weaknesses and find how to deal with them effectively.

# Making Yourself the Priority

Note that self-confidence and self-esteem are harnessed when you accept yourself. Self-love is the balance between taking yourself the way you are, while acknowledging that you deserve better and then working hard toward this. From the above explanation, you will realize that you are the priority. You should make yourself the priority, for the rest of the things to fall in place.

You are not selfish when you prioritize yourself over others. It all depends on the proportions available for sharing. For example, if an orange is cut into four pieces for the four people in the room and you pick two pieces instead of one, that is being selfish. Irrespective of this, it is essential to put yourself first. You must save some energy for yourself at all times.

You are on your own in this world. Therefore, the person with whom you will be in a relationship longer than anyone is yourself. It is when you are in a good relationship with yourself that you will manage your relationships well with other people.

Unfortunately, you have to accept that even though someone may mean well, they may inflict pain on you repeatedly without minding the effect that their action or inaction and words may cause. An ideal situation would be to be in a stable place emotionally, where someone else's actions do not affect your moods.

Therefore, personal growth is an ongoing process, and it may take longer to get to where you're less affected by people's actions. In this case, you are forced to offload those people who bring you down. Some people can be venomous and will restrict your progress so that you cannot even afford a smile. Consider a plant. If placed under harsh conditions, it will not grow and will finally wither. But when placed in the right conditions, the plant will thrive and grow into a beautiful plant. Once it has grown and established its roots and stem, it will be impossible to destroy it.

Human beings can also be toxic. A toxic person is someone who:

- Negatively evaluates all your efforts;

- Demands a lot;
- Disrespects you; and
- Doesn't support your overall objectives.

Such people may:
- Laugh at you;
- Disregard you;
- Abuse you physically;
- Manipulate; and/or
- Belittle you.

These people are often not willing to challenge their harmful actions and make necessary changes. Therefore, when you find yourself around such people who are toxic toward you, you will lose your inner peace. This may force you to transfer the pain inflicted on you to other people. Now it begs the question of whether it is selfish to think of yourself here. Isn't it selfish of them to expect you to be okay with what they do to you?

Ending a bad relationship is hard, since these people may be close to you. But it is important to let go of them, because, once you eliminate those people from your life, you allow for positivity to flow into your life. You will, in the future, have enough time and ample space for self-examination, remedial work, and development, and like the plant we discussed earlier, you will definitely be able to grow.

# Fifteen Proven Ways to Boost Your Self-Confidence

Confidence emanates from within every man. A man's ideas, reflections, and thoughts will help him to build his self-confidence. Below are fifteen proven ways to boost your self-esteem and hence your confidence:

### 1. Be Patient

A confident person must exercise patience. If, as a confident man, you don't attain your goals on the first try, you will not look at it as a failure. You will learn from the experience and strive to do better the next time a similar situation occurs. Patience is a virtue that accompanies persistence. Look at Thomas Edison, who tried inventing the light bulb and failed over 10,000 times. When he asked about his invention, Thomas said that he didn't fail 10,000 times, but instead, he discovered 10,000 ways that didn't work. That shows persistence.

### 2. Love Yourself

As a man, you may think it is wrong to love yourself. You consider it as being selfish, arrogant, and unpleasant. Having this kind of attitude is wrong, since you are mistaking self-love with pride and narcissism. Narcissists don't love themselves. Instead, they are in love with themselves, which is quite different.

Failure to love yourself leads to a reduced sense of self-worth, acceptance, or belonging. Additionally, your capacity to love others is directly affected by your ability to love yourself.

### 3. Overcome Your Fears

Overcoming something that frightens you will make you even stronger and more self-reliant. By overcoming your worries, you will develop an efficient and practical way of dealing with the challenges that you meet in life. It doesn't have to be complicated. Deal with the stress and worries that you face in your daily life. Such an approach increases your self-confidence and sense of self-worth.

Understanding your fears is the initial step to overcoming them. You should understand what threatens you and limits you from achieving your sense of self-worth. Conversely, fear stops you from leaving your comfort zone.

### 4. Have a Mentor

As Joe Montana once stated, confidence is a very fragile thing. This is true. Self-worth needs nurturing and continuous effort to develop it to mature and become an innate part of a man. If you didn't build your self-esteem from your parents' influence, it's not too late. It is time you identified someone you respect in your field and ask them to be your mentor. Many people will accept the request and offer to assist you.

Mentoring should not be confused with life coaching or therapy. Mentoring is merely a process by which you become more knowledgeable and experienced in a particular field; a mentor helps you to navigate the rapids of the path, since he has taken the road himself. Having a mentor in any sector is valuable. You will develop high confidence from the satisfaction that someone is willing to talk to you and guide you as you struggle to make it in life.

### 5. Embrace New Ideas

Embracing new beliefs when you are trying to solve problems is what learning and building self-confidence are all about. You should believe in your resources and those of the people that you trust. If you try to do everything your way, without welcoming new and innovative ideas from others, you are bound to fail.

It is wise to get input from the people surrounding you. Even though sometimes the ideas you require will come from your head, you may end up ignoring them if you have low self-worth. Being open to your thoughts is often a challenge for many men. If you are not open to different ideas from the people around you, your self-confidence will be very low.

### 6. Be Dependable

Knowing that you can count on the people you love, your teammates, and yourself, means you have the tools necessary to get you through rough patches in life. Doing it alone is possible, but it will take you longer. Having others in your life who are dependable always makes things easier, since you will be confident that you don't have to do it all by yourself.

Being dependable may make you more desirable. You will soar higher when people know that they can rely on you. When you realize that you can also rely on yourself, then there is no challenge that you can't handle. Confidence emanates from knowing that you or the person you need will be there when you need them.

### 7. Practice Positive Thinking

You may often say negative things about yourself. When this becomes a habit, it prevents you from enjoying life, achieving your objectives, or sometimes it hampers you from finding love. One of the ways to break the habit of negative thinking is to be aware of negative thoughts. Being conscious of what is going on in your head and around you, will help you to reduce the tension.

### 8. Avoid Procrastination

Put all the excuses away and acknowledge that you have the capacity to complete the task on time. Many men would prefer to accomplish the task at the last minute. Procrastination is a bad habit that must be eliminated for you to develop your self-confidence. To achieve this:

✔ Start timing everything, to find out how long it takes you to do something that you have been dragging on.

✔ Just do it. If you start and work on the task at hand, you will eventually have some time later on that you can utilize in any manner.

✔ Conquer your fears—some men avoid tasks for fear of failing at implementing them. This fear is an excuse that will lead you to delay or completely ignore essential things in life.

✔ Plan your free time. Always reward yourself by giving yourself a break once you have attained your milestones. Breaks are vital; you cannot be productive for the entire day. Resting makes you sharp.

### 9. Respond Promptly

Responding to problems rather than reacting will save you a lot of pain. Some fear may drive you to go into reaction mode. This reaction can be triggered by anxiety. To handle situations efficiently, you must learn to respond. It takes practice to stop reacting to matters and instead respond promptly to them. You should discuss these processes with someone you trust and believe in. This way, you can help each other to avoid reactions and seek appropriate responses.

## 10. Exercise Your Mental Strength

Take, for example, a game of chess. Someone who has won a chess game, or succeeded at chess, has spent many hours practicing. There are many ways to exercise your mental strength. The advantage of mental exercise is that it can be done anywhere, while you are running your day to day life. But remember, this is not one solution that fits all. What works with one person may not work with another.

## 11. Strengthen Your Support Structure

Support structures have been in existence even before the coming of psychotherapy. It is essential to have people around you who are willing to hold your hand through the challenges that life throws at you. In case you don't have friends, family, or colleagues who offer you emotional support, you can join a group that does so. Alternatively, you can create your own support group.

You can get emotional support from such groups. The help you can get from support groups will not only build your confidence but will also set you on the pathway toward living a fruitful life.

## 12. Celebrate Small Achievements

You don't have to be successful to be confident. Many have proven the opposite. When you develop success in any sector of your life, it will affect all the other areas of your life. Little achievements can be anything from running a few kilometers every day. You can set realistic targets for the number of kilometers you would wish to cover in a day. Once you have achieved the small goals, you should celebrate your achievements. Your self-worth will gradually increase as you appreciate the small wins in your life.

## 13. Keep Fit and Healthy

A healthy man will have the confidence to accomplish any task and face any challenge that life throws at him. If you are not healthy, even surviving will become a problem. Being fit is necessary for your self-esteem and physical well-being. Fitness can be achieved easily by exercising. Being healthy and assisting others to be healthy is essential to enable you to live a fulfilling life. When you are out of shape or are unhealthy, the mere basics of life will be hard for you to achieve; hence you will suffer from low self-worth.

### 14. Practice Giving

Assisting others will help you to know that you are a nice person and that you can have a positive impact on society. When things are tough, giving money to a worthy cause or volunteering may seem counterproductive. Even with the pressures of life, people still find ways to give. Giving money makes you feel good about yourself, hence boosting your self-confidence. By providing a little something to someone in need, even just your time and care, you build self-respect, since you believe you have contributed to making the world a better place.

### 15. Avoid Critical Comments

When you say something hurtful to someone, you will end up pushing them away to the point that they will not want to connect with you ever again. Here, your emotional support structures are damaged. When you regularly criticize someone, the person to whom you are directing the criticism may just be acting along to manage your tantrums. Even if you are trying to help them, you will be turning them away. Once your advice is ignored, you will feel that you are not respected. Being ignored will not be good for your self-confidence.

To avoid this negative energy, carefully think of the words you use. Before saying them out loud, imagine how you would feel if the words were directed to you; if you get upset, so will everybody else. By interacting in a manner that does not offend others or make them feel judged or held down, they will also open-up and share their opinions.

# Like a Boss: Six Workplace Confidence Hacks

Confidence is an essential component in a workplace environment. Can you imagine a workplace full of employees with low self-esteem? Would you prefer working or even seeking services from such an entity? Confidence in the workplace involves assisting people in understanding their emotions.

Smart goals and tight deadlines define a work environment. Therefore, your self-confidence will increase if you can meet the deadlines and deliver a quality job performance at the end of the day.

Napoleon Hill once stated: "What the mind can conceive and believe, it can achieve." In this section, we will discuss the workplace mindset that men should adopt. While you are trying to manifest your objectives, it is crucial to keep a high vibration.

In a work setting, feelings are often exchanged among colleagues on a like-for-like basis. Therefore, you need to master everything you have learned in the previous section of this book about self-confidence and self-esteem. However, without a doubt, your belief is pivotal as far as manifestation is concerned. This means if you don't believe in something, you will not see it occurring in your life. In this section, we will explore how our beliefs affect our workplace performance and the quality of relationships in the office.

## The Six Workplace Self-Confidence Hacks

Below are six workplace confidence hacks that you must know to navigate the work environment like a boss:

### Hack 1: Practice Positive Thinking in Your Job Situation

Here, positive thinking refers to the practice of choosing ideas that will empower you over those that will limit you. In the workplace, a positive mind will give you a positive life.

A positive mind is superior to a negative mind in the sense that positive thinking entails selecting the thoughts and actions that support the project rather than hampering it, and it eventually brings the best outcome irrespective of the situation.

Harboring negative thoughts like "You can't do it," will prevent you from taking necessary steps toward achieving your objectives. You will then be less likely to meet the set goals.

Positive thoughts like "You can do it," will enable you to try, therefore, increasing your chances of meeting your own goals.

A negative thought process will restrict you, while a positive one will move you closer to your goals within the workplace. When you believe that something is impossible, it will mean that the barriers to success have absorbed you completely.

You should maintain a positive attitude in the workplace. A positive attitude will give you hope and, at the same time, change your perspective. In the workplace environment, you need to find people who have succeeded in what you're doing and learn from them. Your thoughts will help you move up the ranks at your workplace—or they will pull you back. Also, acknowledge that it's never too late to transform your ideas and transform your beliefs to support rather than obstruct yourself.

### Hack 2: Workplace Mentality Is Your Reality

Henry Ford once quoted that: "Whether you think you can or think you can't, you are right."

Another philosopher called Immanuel Kant said that our experiences, including sensations and our perception of objects, are representations of our mind. And that reality is only based on an individual's perception.

Your perception of the workplace is dependent on your self-beliefs. These beliefs are your truths that build your subjective realities toward workplace self-confidence. A belief, here, is the feeling of certainty toward something—your lives and jobs are based on the beliefs you acquire through your experiences.

At your job, it's necessary that your personal growth is open to the beliefs of others and that you are willing to change your beliefs if convinced that an alternative way of looking at things will provide a more accurate and empowering solution.

### Hack 3: Listening to Your Subconscious Mind

Within your job environment, it is vital to engage and understand the signals coming from your subconscious mind. Your limiting beliefs are among those continually taking root in your subconscious, since they are repeatedly planted there. The subconscious mind doesn't evaluate the ideas. It slowly transforms our beliefs. This means that, if you are fearful, jealous, and power-hungry, you will always sow bad seeds in yours and other minds, which will, in turn, limit your potential in life.

### Hack 4: Analyzing Your Thoughts

If you cannot change a situation, try to change your view of it. That's where your power is. Either be controlled—or be in control. Your brain is intelligent. It wants to make life easy for you and to do as little thinking as possible. (This might sound a little strange, especially if you're a chronic overthinker.) So, the brain is optimized to make subconscious decisions based on previous emotions attached to experiences. This autopilot behavior brought about by repetition enables you to move through your day without having to relearn processes, such as driving, and without having to think through all the minutiae of daily life.

However, since your subconscious mind has no awareness, it can unwittingly hold you captive to unhealthy behavior. The fact that you felt terrible every time you reacted violently to abuse you may have been subjected to, for example, should make you realize that it wasn't your conscious reaction. You were conditioned to respond like that by your past experiences, and you didn't question your response because you think you lack awareness.

How you view an event determines how you experience it. Facts are neutral, but you often give them labels. When an unfortunate event happens, pause, and observe your thoughts. By doing this, your unconscious mind will replace thought with awareness. Only once you discover your thoughts, will you choose how to respond. Meditation is a powerful tool for enhancing this skill.

In summary, instead of trying to control events that are external to you, practice controlling your mind's response to them. Controlling the mind gives you back your power and is the key to a happy life. Therefore, in a workplace environment, your ultimate objective is not to just get rid of the limiting thoughts, but to analyze them first.

**Hack 5: Changing Your Limiting Beliefs**

It would be good to change your beliefs faster, but this is a difficult thing to achieve. Your beliefs are engraved in your subconscious mind. When you accept a notion without question, you live with it your entire life. Some ideas will make sense to you, but they will not empower you. They will only limit your potential in life and your ability to attain your objectives.

The first step is to identify the beliefs that you wish to change. For instance, let's say that one of your core beliefs is that you cannot change your future, so you won't be able to accomplish great things.

These beliefs won't make you feel good, but if you'd tried to change them right away, you would have felt as though you were lying to yourself. After all, these beliefs were your truth. But why did you *think* they were the truth?

When you confront your limiting beliefs, you will discover that you believed what you did because someone told you. These limiting beliefs that were passed onto you by some other people should be avoided at all costs.

### Hack 6: Continuous Affirmation

Never underestimate the power of affirmations. These are the positive statements that describe what your goals and objectives are in life, as if you have already achieved them. Repeating something with great conviction generates a belief in your subconscious that the statement is true.

It is common in society. You are often fed certain notions about the world, which are repeated over and over again. For instance, let's say your parents continually told you that you were shy; all that happened was this was reinforced in your mind. You may not feel shy. But, through repetition of this idea, you might start believing it. Consequently, you will grow up to be shy—here, these words become a self-fulfilling prophecy.

This should remind you of the importance of surrounding yourself with people who are feeding you with empowering thoughts. This is not to say that you should only keep friends who say good things about you. But it does mean that you should pick people who are supportive, not destructive to your life's objectives.

When you are repeatedly told that you can't do something, you will end up believing that it is true. Repeating positive affirmations is a conscious process. When you send instructions to your subconscious mind, once these beliefs are planted, your subconscious mind will do all it can to bring these ideas to life. It's like coding a program to do something for you. Once the codes are correctly done, the program will deliver its intended purpose.

Repeating positive affirmations is useful in life. You can practice saying your affirmations at a time when you are feeling okay. At this stage, they will gain momentum faster by you repeating these affirmations. This habit will change your state of mind and belief systems, and as such, your reality, completely.

Practice saying affirmations in your own words and voice like telling irrefutable facts to your friend. Care should be taken only to repeat positive statements—don't recite limiting comments. You should act in a manner suggesting that the goal has already been achieved. This way, the subconscious will believe and will respond accordingly. It is upon you to allocate more time for regularly reciting positive affirmations.

# Dating Confidence: Twelve Irresistible Strategies to Win Her Over

If you have picked this book, you are probably like many men out there. You have trouble and trepidation when it comes to winning women, especially when it comes to flirting and trying to get her into bed. It's a common issue for men, and not every man is a natural when it comes to charm and seduction. But it doesn't mean you cannot succeed when it comes to winning women.

Confidence is critical when it comes to women. It is an aphrodisiac to women. Women can detect confidence, since it is what they look for in a man. Dating has become a killer of men's confidence. You may even find it hard to ask a woman out for a date. You may wonder:

✔ How do you get yourself to make that move?

✔ How do you get to look her straight in the eye and make your request?

The ability to have control over sex and your love life, in many ways, defines who you are. The ability to win ladies improves your internal happiness and self-worth. When you succeed in winning women, you will reap the benefits of your masculine ambition and trust in your abilities. This will consequently boost your self-confidence.

What you need to know is how to increase your chances of success in relationships. Here are twelve strategies that can get you started, in an attempt at winning over a romantic prospect:

### 1. Be Committed to the Cause

Here, you should take committed action to win her over, even if the response is negative. You should keep asking women out and detach yourself from the negative outcome. Don't blame yourself or look down upon yourself when the answer is always negative after several trials. It can take you over a year to get the first date. All you need to do is to stay committed to the course and if one person isn't interested, you will eventually find a match who is right for you.

### 2. Know Yourself

Here, you should establish whether you are gay, bisexual, straight, or not identified at all. You must determine which side you are on and accept who you are. When you know and accept yourself, you will interact easily with others. Learning to communicate efficiently with ladies and getting them to like you will help you to achieve your objective of self-confidence. You must be the kind of person you want to attract.

### 3. Be Yourself

After you have known yourself and accepted yourself, you should just be yourself. Do not struggle to be someone else; it's tough to keep up an act. Never give her a wrong impression of who you are, or act in a way that you cannot maintain. Ladies will fall for you if you don't exaggerate your abilities by struggling hard to impress them instead of being real.

### 4. Gain Confidence Before Approaching Her

In meeting women, you will always find that those men who are confident are more successful. This has nothing to do with good luck.

Women prefer you to be a confident person, not meek and unsure of yourself. Women don't like men who stand aloof and look at them secretly. Whether it is for a one-night stand or long-term, women will not consider dating a loser.

You need the confidence to approach women. When you know how to talk to women and have the right attitude, you will start to exude self-assurance. With more confidence and plenty of practice, you will find that the techniques in this book can help you to hook up with any girl you want.

### 5. Keep Practicing

Always practice, practice, and practice—again and again. One of the biggest mistakes that you can make in this endeavor is to start by talking to the most beautiful woman in the room.

If you are not used to doing this, you will start doubting yourself. Hence trouble will begin here because you will be making excuses right away as to why you can't approach someone. These doubts arise because you haven't invested in talking with many women to be confident enough to approach the one that you have genuinely fallen in love with.

Therefore, like any sector in life, continuous practice will help you perfect it. You will build your confidence slowly. You will begin having conversations with women—just talking, with no expectations. This includes people you are not attracted to.

Once you practice persistently, your confidence will grow, and it will be easier to start conversations with random women. With time, you will have no problem walking across that crowded room and picking the beautiful lady who has attracted you.

### 6. Pick a Good Dating Location

Another great tip to help you meet the type of women that you would like, and that will make it easier to converse with them, is to choose a type of venue that makes you feel at home. Perhaps you don't like the bar or club scene, for example. This could make approaching women in these locations more difficult if you hate yelling over the music or looking like a fool on the dance floor— unless, of course, you know how to dance.

Instead of using that as an avenue for meeting women, consider classes, such as an art class or a cooking class, head to the park, a farmer's market or grocery store, a museum. Find those locations that you enjoy, and you will find that you are more comfortable and confident when it comes to approaching women and talking with them.

### 7. Always Keep Learning

Building your confidence is a vital initial step. You can always learn new things: being curious and open to new experiences and constant learning is key.

### 8. Be Humorous, Hygienic, and Always Smile

These are essential aspects for you to develop before hitting on a lady. Sure, you want to get out there and meet women who are going to be interested in you and who will want to sleep with you. However, all of the talking in the world is not going to get you anywhere if you are humorless, gruff, and hygiene-challenged. Think about it from the woman's perspective for a bit. Would you want to go home with someone who did not take care of themselves, and who was grim most of the time? Probably not.

That's why this chapter is all about working on yourself and making yourself into a better catch before you start trying to hook up with women. By taking these steps now and making some improvements in your life, you will find that it can help you to build the confidence discussed in the first chapter. You are going to be happier with who you are and what you have to offer.

You will exude confidence, and that's what so many women find attractive, whether they are looking for a one-night stand or someone with whom they can build a real relationship.

### 9. Upgrade Your Overall Physical Appearance

We're not talking about running out and getting plastic surgery to look like whoever the current heartthrob actor or musician is right now. It's far more straightforward than that, fortunately. You will find that even if you are an average guy, or perhaps even a somewhat less than average guy, there are plenty of things you can do that will help to change and improve your physical appearance to make you more attractive.

## 10. Keep Fit

Your physical fitness is a vital aspect of enhancing your confidence and consequently landing the woman of your dreams. The first step is to make sure that you are taking good care of yourself when it comes to your physical fitness. Not only is it essential for your health, but it is crucial to how women perceive you. If you are hoping to sleep with good-looking women with beautiful bodies, you can be sure they want something equivalent from the men they choose.

Whether you are overweight, flabby, or nothing but skin, bones, and a little bit of muscle, you can do better. If you have some resources, spend some money and time to shed some pounds and build muscle. You don't need to have a six-pack, and you don't need to look like a fitness model. You need to make sure you are in shape and that you look good.

For many men, the journey to fitness might be longer than it is for others. Perhaps you've neglected taking care of yourself for a while now, or maybe fitness was never necessary to you. Now is the time to start getting into great shape. You are going to feel better, and you are going to look better. When this happens, you are going to be bursting with energy and confidence.

The fitness requirements will entirely depend on the body you wish to acquire, whether you are trying to lose weight or build your muscles. Some men may be skinny and may want to add some muscles. To achieve this, you can go to the gym if you have an affordable one in your area. You can also consider hiking, swimming, walking, or running. You need not spend a lot of money getting into good shape. Calisthenics and bodyweight exercises can transform your body.

The goal of this book is not to give you a bunch of workout plans that you can use. Instead, it will teach you how to pick and choose relationships with women. Getting into shape is just one of the aspects you will have to consider.

Just make sure you follow through with the proposed exercise plan and put in the necessary time and effort required to get into shape before you begin trying to strut around a club picking up women. The better shape you are in, the easier it will be to win women.

## 11. Dress to Impress

In addition to getting your body into shape, you need to think about other aspects of your outward appearance. This certainly includes the clothes and shoes that you are wearing.

People say that you should never judge a book by its cover. However, it's human nature to do just that. People judge based on appearances, and there's nothing you can do about that. If you were to see an unkempt woman in ragged, dirty sweatpants, wearing an old baggy t-shirt, and with a cigarette dangling out of her mouth, you are probably not going to think she's the most attractive woman in the room.

Now, think about it from a woman's perspective. If you have holes in your clothes, ratty shoes with frayed laces, and stains on your clothes that just won't come off, why would she be interested? You can't wear your favorite Velcro sneakers everywhere, no matter how comfy they might feel. You are not a professional hobo, so don't dress like it.

Sure, if you are lounging around the house, wear whatever you want. Be comfortable. When you head out, though, whether you are heading to the gym, to work, to the store, or you are going out to a bar, movie, museum, or anywhere else, dress appropriately.

You should not spend all your money on new clothing. You probably have a few things around the house that you can wear that look good, and that make you feel great about yourself. That last bit is the most important. You want clothes that work well for you and that make you look as good as possible.

Maybe you do need to spend a bit of money getting some clothes that fit better to your body shape. This is undoubtedly true if you have been working out and getting into better shape, as mentioned. If you aren't sure exactly what you should be wearing to look good or the type of clothing that will work best for you, seek help from some friends.

If you have some friends who are women—and hopefully you do—they can provide you with some great suggestions. If you aren't sure who you should be asking, then you can always spend some time talking with people in the clothing shop. They can certainly help, but don't fall into the trap of buying shoes and clothing items that are more expensive than you need.

Now that you have started to think about your physical fitness and health, and you've started to look at your wardrobe to see what you need to buy, it's time that we talked about hygiene.

## 12. Work on Your Hygiene

If you are an adult who has managed to get through your awkward teenage years, you should have at least a basic grounding of cleanliness and know how important it truly is if you want to attract women. However, it does still bear repeating here because there are plenty of men—too many, in fact—out there who do not care one iota about grooming.

It doesn't matter if it's just a one-night stand or a long-term relationship. If you stink with fuzzy teeth and untamed hair, you aren't going to win women. And you should not. Take proper care of your hygiene.

Get into a routine for hygiene and stick to it. Honestly, it's straightforward, and it might amaze you how many men don't seem to care. Here are some simple yet vital grooming and hygiene tips and reminders for men.

✔ **Wear deodorant.** Wear it every damned day, and maybe add some twice a day if you need it. You want a pleasant fragrance for the deodorant and antiperspirant, but not something that is going to be overwhelming.

✔ **Wash your face.** You should wash your face twice per day. Washing helps to make sure that your face is clean and is not going to break out. Stay away from using soap, body scrubs, and body gels on the face, as these can dry and irritate the skin. Use a facial cleanser instead.

✔ **Brush your teeth.** You want to brush your teeth three times per day. Do it in the morning after breakfast, after lunch, and before you head to bed. This will keep the teeth in good shape, and it helps you to maintain a white smile. I'd recommend activated charcoal by teethwhiteningsolutions.com. Your smile is essential, as you'll see later in this section.

✔ **Floss.** Brushing is essential, but don't forget just how important it is to floss, as well. Floss at least once per day, as well as whenever you feel as though something might be stuck between your teeth. If you plan to kiss a woman, you need to make sure your teeth and breath are on point. Otherwise, it's going to be a no go.

✔ **Change your underpants.** Sure, you should change your underwear daily. But do we always do this? Are there days where you say, "That's okay" and head outside? Remember always to change your underwear after a workout. Dirty underclothes are a major turnoff to ladies.

✔ **Wash your clothes.** Just because you sniff your shirts or pants and don't think they stink, and you don't see any stains, does not mean they are clean. Get into the habit of washing your clothes regularly and hang and fold them properly so that they do not get any wrinkles.

✔ **Shower at least once or twice a day.** You should ideally shower in the morning before you head out, as well as at night after a long day. Wash once a day at the very least. Besides, make sure that you shower after you have been working out. It's better for your skin, and it ensures you don't have any leftover funk on you after the gym. If you are going to be going out where you could meet someone—which is just about anywhere—make sure you are clean and fresh before you leave the house.

✔ **Clip your nails.** Take a look at your fingernails and then your toenails. Having trimmed nails is something that women often look for when they are talking to a man that piques their interest. If the nails are long enough to hold dirt, then they are too long. If the toenails are starting to curl over at the edges, then they are far too long. No, this doesn't mean that you need to invest in a manicure or pedicure. It just means you need to take a minute each day to check your nails and make sure they aren't out of hand.

✔ **Shave or trim the beard.** Having facial hair is okay, provided you keep it groomed and trimmed properly. Use beard oil and other products to make sure it is in good shape, and to make sure it doesn't stink. Yes, some men have bushy beards that stink, and that's going to be a big turn off for most women. When it comes to having facial hair, something else that you will want to remember is that not all women like it. By having a beard or a mustache, you are limiting the number of women who may immediately find you attractive. Think about whether you need a beard or not.

✔ **Groom below the neck and the belt.** you should keep in mind that you want to groom your entire body, including where she can't see when you first meet. You must consider grooming the pubic area when you do find a woman to sleep with.

The simple tips above will help you stand out above many men.

# Taming Your Overconfidence

Developing self-confidence is a good thing. But in excess, it can be detrimental to your personal growth and even kill your self-esteem and, consequently, your self-worth. Overconfidence occurs when you are excessively confident or overly optimistic about yourself. This may be hazardous to your self-worth and overall well-being.

An overly confident man will cause more trouble than he solves problems. Overconfidence will kill your creativity and will lead you into a downward spiral. If you are overconfident, you may ignore advice from your peers, family, and colleagues, because you believe you can handle everything yourself, and you are convinced that your ability is enough to handle the situation at hand.

Taming your confidence is essential; you should maintain confidence levels that are within acceptable thresholds. The need to be better than the rest and to be recognized for what you do at the expense of others is a clear sign of overconfidence. There is a thin line separating overconfidence and arrogance. Overconfidence is the enemy of what you want and what you have. Overconfidence can cause you to lose everything you have worked tirelessly for over the years.

Overconfidence is the voice within that tells you that you are better than you are; it inhibits real success and prevents a direct and honest connection to the society around you. It is a conscious separation from everything. It prevents us from working collaboratively with other people.

You should suppress overconfidence early enough before the bad habits that come with it become innate. Overconfidence will forever impede your aspirations. Taming your overconfidence is a journey that will take longer, depending on how damaged your self-worth is. Many men are struggling unnecessarily, simply because they don't realize that overconfidence is causing the problems they are facing in life. You should be able to recognize overconfidence or ego and how to get it under control.

You can manage your confidence levels. But how do you know for sure if it has reached a level that you have to tame? Here are some signs that you need to work on your overconfidence:

- You are never satisfied with your accomplishments—you find yourself working toward a goal, telling yourself that once you reach it, you will be a happy man, and live a fulfilled life. But once you do, you remain unhappy. This is a sign of overconfidence and a damaged ego.

- You are always insecure and envious of others—this is depicted when you have the constant need to compare yourself to others to find satisfaction. You are never okay with where you are unless you are convinced that it is better than where someone else is. You derive happiness from knowing that you are smarter or better than others.

- You burn bridges on your way—this can be a long list of bad breakups, friendships falling apart after an argument, et cetera. These are signs that your confidence level is out of control. If you have trouble keeping healthy relationships, it means you are confident that you can work things out alone, and this is a limiting belief.

- You exhibit a lot of addiction to social media—overconfidence thrives on the instant gratification of social media. If you find yourself always reaching for something like your smartphone, it's a likely sign that your confidence level needs some work.

If these points apply to you, you will be required to tame your overconfidence. The good news is that it is possible to tame your overconfidence. All it needs is commitment. If you are willing to improve your life, self-worth, relationships, and your self-confidence, this book is perfect for you. It will give you practical advice to taming your overconfidence.

Overconfidence causes you to be arrogant. Confidence that we have discussed in the previous chapters is different from the arrogance that is depicted by overconfidence. You can be excessively confident about your skills or abilities. You may accept yourself completely without becoming arrogant in your interactions with others.

Some people will argue that overconfidence is not a bad thing. The same people would say that overconfidence is necessary to succeed. The idea of succeeding, in this example, would mean winning status, honor, and attaining material possessions or prestige. It is only when your confidence is enormous that you will be able to succeed on particular job paths or get to the top of the chain. For instance, in jobs where harming others is mandatory, reaching the top would mean sacrificing your respect of others for the sake of serving your overconfidence.

# Ten Habits Necessary for Taming Overconfidence

Since your confidence levels are complicated and are multi-leveled, it is not practical to get rid of it all at once. It is not even humanly possible to achieve that. Below are habits that you can practice to tame your overconfidence:

## 1. Have Realistic Expectations for Your Confidence and Personal Goals

This will not happen instantly, and if you have unrealistic expectations you will only cause yourself unnecessary heartache. Instead, commit to improving yourself gradually, every day in small chunks—provided you are moving forward every day.

You can view the process of getting rid of limiting beliefs and destructive mental habits in the same way as removing a burdensome tree from the garden. Begin by identifying thoughts that exist to strengthen your overconfidence, and then detach from them, eventually getting to a place where you can let them go, seeing yourself as separate from the fake identity that your overconfidence brought about.

## 2. Practice Meditation

This is the leading method for noticing your overconfidence and separating yourself from it. Meditation is a great way to detach from habits that promote overconfidence. A number of religions sing the praises of meditation frequently, and for a good reason, since it pays off immensely to those who commit to it—you don't need to be religious to benefit.

## 3. Noticing Your Thoughts

Meditation, contrary to popular belief and rumor, isn't about trying to stop thinking. It's about learning to see your ideas. Once you begin to do this, you will see that most of these thoughts that cross your mind throughout the day seem to come out of nowhere, and many of them don't even make sense.

## 4. Eliminating the Constant Stream of Nonsense

You don't choose your thoughts, which is why advertising is a successful business. You are subjected to hundreds of things each day, often against your will, and this is even more apparent in the era of social media. How many times per day do you find yourself thinking of some random nonsense that you saw earlier and don't care about at all? The good news is that you don't have to be subjected to this, mindfulness will help you to tune out the excess "noise" from these sources.

### 5. Blocking Unworthy Thoughts

The idea here is not to stop the thoughts completely but to address them when they show up. With meditation, you can realize these thoughts when they manifest and accept then move past the ones that aren't worth your time.

### 6. Harnessing Empowering Thoughts

An average person is tossed around all day long by this cascade of thoughts, and meditation gives you back the power to be the one in control. You will start to recognize when your ego starts to try to take over, and you will be giving yourself the option of saying no.

### 7. Find a Creative Pursuit

Creativity is an excellent source of inspiration that can disengage you from the constant chatter of your confidence levels. People often believe that they are "not creative," but this isn't true. Every person is creative, and the only thing holding you back from thinking this is your overconfident tendencies.

### 8. Taking a Walk in Nature

Humans in modern times live in an unnatural environment and rarely see the outdoors. This leads to a lot of discomfort that you often don't even realize. To neutralize the overconfidence levels and become a healthier, more grounded individual, you must regain contact with your roots as a member of this planet and start going outside more.

### 9. Spend Some Time with Children

Children have less developed confidence levels, so they are truer and more themselves, something many adults have forgotten. Hanging out with them can really help you to begin thinking in a clearer and simpler way about what is really important in life.

### 10. Decluttering

Owning a lot of stuff is not a bad thing, but it can weigh on you, and pull you down, and intensify your overconfidence. It's too easy to start equating your own sense of worth with what you own when you have a lot of stuff. You become afraid of what would happen if you didn't have these things. In other words, you fear that the false confidence that you've built up would cease to exist if you didn't have the material possessions. When you offload some of the possessions, you will become less worried about material things, and at the same time, you will enjoy giving others the things you no longer need.

# PART 3: Self-Discipline

# Self-Discipline and Its Core Values

Self-discipline is the control you exert over yourself. For example, the power you have over your emotions, feelings, behaviors, activities, and even what you think. It entails avoiding unhealthy excesses that may result in negative consequences. If you are a self-disciplined man, you will easily control your urges to indulge in harmful or unconstructive activities that may negatively affect your productivity. You tend to stick to your mission and objectives.

From this definition, you may confuse self-discipline with willpower. Willpower is the ability to set a course of action and be sure that you will start it and manage it to the end. You can control any damaging or needless impulses, and have the ability to overcome procrastination and laziness, as well as the ability to arrive at a decision then follow through with perseverance to its logical end.

Self-discipline differs from this in the sense that willpower will get you started in setting your goals and remaining on course. But self-discipline is required if you wish to realize your true potential in life. Once willpower has placed you on the road, you need something to keep you going, and that is self-discipline. It gives you the stamina to persevere in whatever you do. It gives you the strength to withstand hardships, be they emotional or mental. Also, self-discipline gives you the ability to reject instant gratification for the greater good in the long run. This may require a lot of effort and time. Therefore, you will realize that there is a very thin line between self-discipline and willpower.

To develop a strong sense of discipline and willpower, you will become conscious of your internal subconscious impulses and gain the ability to discard them anytime they are not for your benefit. In essence, self-discipline coupled with strong willpower allows you to choose your behavior and reactions, instead of being enslaved by them. You feel more powerful and in charge of yourself and your surroundings when you muster self-discipline.

Self-discipline is critically essential if you want to get things done promptly, mainly because it helps you stay on the path to achieving your goals. So how can you build your self-discipline? Well, before we start discussing various ways and methods you can use to develop this ability, it is essential first to explain the reasons why most of us lack this key ability. Delving into these two aspects will help you understand the importance of developing self-confidence.

## Six Reasons Why You Need Self-Discipline

The core value of self-discipline is success. Therefore, it is important to exercise discipline at every opportunity. Reasons for harnessing self-discipline in your life include:

>**1.** Lack of it will mean you lack self-control. Thus, when working on something, you quickly get distracted and give in to your desires, urges, and feelings. You do not stay dedicated to your missions, and you quickly lose sight of what is essential and beneficial to you. Self-discipline seeks to reverse that; it helps you to stick to whatever it is you have planned to do, no matter the level of discomfort or difficulties that you face along the way.

When self-discipline is lacking, your chances of becoming sidetracked are high, meaning that you can forget long-term desires and goals forever. On the contrary, if you practice self-discipline, you will always achieve everything you desire in life.

2. Self-discipline will enable you to exercise control over yourself and avoid thinking or feeling negative. When you are self-disciplined, you think before acting, brainstorm quickly, think lucidly, focus on essential tasks, efficiently complete all the chores you have started, and successfully carry out your plans and decisions despite obstacles, hardships, and inconveniences that come your way.

3. Additionally, self-discipline helps you to make the right choices by evaluating things, by weighing their pros and cons; when you are self-disciplined, you seldom make erratic impulsive decisions.

4. Furthermore, self-discipline helps you to become happier and more peaceful. A study titled: *Yes, But Are They Happy? Effects of Trait Self-Control on Affective Well-Being and Life Satisfaction,* was conducted in 2013 by Wilhelm Hoffman, and showed that those who had high self-control were happier as compared to those who lacked self-control. According to the study, self-disciplined people deal with their goal conflicts a lot better, waste less time in unhealthy behaviors, and can make positive decisions easily. This, in turn, enhances their levels of inner peace and happiness.

5. Self-discipline can help you to avoid making decisions in a rash or an impulsive manner, making you fulfill promises that you set for yourself and others, and continue working on a project even when your enthusiasm has faded away. It is the one thing that will make you wake up every single morning to do some of the things that you feel you shouldn't be doing because of your lack of enthusiasm.

6. With self-discipline, you can build healthy relationships, command respect from others, and you can also manage your

thoughts, reactions, and eventually achieve everything you have set your eyes and mind to.

From the above, it is clear that nurturing habits that enhance your self-discipline is the right step toward transforming your life.

## Why Men Lack Self-Discipline

Even though self-discipline is a vital element that should be part of your personality, many men lack it and are extremely far from acquiring it. Ask yourself what makes it so impossible for you to overcome laziness, stop excessive eating, or stop smoking?

The answer is you don't have the self-discipline to do what should be done to realize your goals and desires. You need to know what is lacking to correctly address the situation. Here are the reasons why self-discipline may be lacking:

- **Self-Discipline Is Not a Built-In Ability**

Self-discipline is not something you are born with; it is something you work on and develop. Those who are disciplined have worked hard to build this strength and those who do not have it need to put in the effort to acquire it.

- **Negative Mental and Emotional Programming**

Not all of us have positive and healthy "mental programming." In childhood and throughout their lives, many people go through various terrible incidents that induce negative thinking, which shapes negative behaviors and keeps them from gaining self-discipline.

- **Negative Environments**

A positive environment is mandatory in the development of self-discipline and willpower. If the people around you are not supportive and constantly demoralize you, you will never be able to discern right and wrong and discipline yourself. If you are not lucky enough to reside in a positive environment, you need to work on creating one for yourself to gain self-discipline.

- **Fear of Failure**

The fear of failing at something prevents you from taking the initiative. When you cannot initiate tasks and activities, you cannot move toward your goals. This lowers your inner strength, an integral and essential part of developing willpower.

- **Laziness**

If you are incredibly lazy, you never feel like doing anything and are always procrastinating. Where there is procrastination, there cannot be self-discipline. To develop self-discipline, laziness and procrastination have to go: it is that simple.

- **Low Self-Esteem and Self-Confidence**

When you are not sure of yourself and do not highly value yourself, you cannot be confident of your abilities. When you are not aware of your strengths and lack confidence, developing the discipline to get things done will be a challenge. It is harder to develop the skills you need, because if you have low self-esteem and confidence, it will seem much easier to procrastinate even if the task is critical to your attainment of certain goals.

- **Easily Falling Prey to Temptation**

If you easily fall prey to different things that lure you away from your goal, your self-discipline is lacking. To gain restraint and self-will, it is essential to overcome your weaknesses and temptations.

- **A Lack of Purpose**

To be self-disciplined, your life must have a purpose, a goal you look forward to, and that you can stay dedicated to. On the contrary, if you do not know your lifelong objectives, and have not realized them yet, you are likely to be lacking self-discipline.

From the above, you have now noticed one or two reasons why your self-discipline is wanting. Lack of self-discipline reduces your chances of achieving whatever it is you wish to achieve in life. Therefore, self-discipline is a quality that you must adopt in your life.

# Mindset Matters: Changing Your Limiting Beliefs

This section will show you the power of your beliefs. You may be aware of these beliefs or not, but either way, limiting beliefs affect what your goals are in life. Changing your self-limiting views, even in the simplest way possible, can have positive effects on your self-confidence.

Your personality emanates from your mindset. Everything that is preventing you from fulfilling your set objectives is based on your beliefs and mindset.

Muhammad Yunus once said: "My greatest challenge has been to change the mindset of people." He goes on to say that, "Mindsets play strange tricks on us. We see things the way our minds have instructed our eyes to see."

Everyone has a biased view of the world. This is because your childhood experiences have shaped your beliefs in life, how you see things, and how you perceive reality. For example, if you lived in poverty all your life, with sexual and emotional abuse, you will never believe in the goodness that life can bring until you choose to do so.

This means that your thoughts are a significant factor that affect your mindset and how you view life. For example, you may not have grown up in a hardship neighborhood, but you saw a friend or neighbor who was once prosperous, suddenly becoming poor in a snap. This will make you think and believe that it is possible to rise and fall quickly. When you think a lot about it, you will fear that it may happen to you. And gradually, you will start believing in it, and your mind will start looking for ways to make the belief come to pass.

You may not be able to control a lot that happens in your life, but one thing you can control is your thoughts. Your subconscious mind can't quickly tell the difference between what is real and what is an illusion created by your imagination. The mind will accept the input you give it and will act accordingly to process those inputs.

Here, the decision is yours. This section will help you to decide whether you will continue to hold on to the wrong mindset about yourself—by continuing to let the world or your past shape your confidence—or you will act to improve it. If you wish to change your mindset, below are some of the negative beliefs that you need to get rid of before installing new views:

## Three Bad Mindsets That You Should Avoid

- Perfection

This is one of the wrong mindsets to have, as it can reduce your self-confidence. A misconception is that you are good only when you are "perfect." Of course, you will not be confident when you mess up something, but it doesn't mean that you can't develop self-confidence. Perfectionism can compromise your self-esteem. If you peg your confidence on "being perfect," it means you will never be confident in your entire life, because no one is perfect.

- That a Mindset is Permanent

You may believe that your fate is cast in stone and that you cannot change anything about yourself. You tend to have the mindset that this is just: "How God made you." Such a statement shows that your situation is permanent and that it cannot be changed. This limiting belief will make you feel like a lesser being. With such low self-esteem, it will prevent you from becoming confident about yourself. If you have such a fixed mindset, you will often think that striving to be self-confident is a waste of time. Affected men will avoid anything that requires extreme effort to change for the better.

- **Achievement Equals Confidence**

Your achievements can, indeed, make you confident. But this should not be confused to mean that you have first to achieve in order to be confident. On the contrary, you may realize so much success in life, only because you were confident in the first place. If you achieve without confidence, that is considered an accidental achievement. Take an example of the late Kobe Bryant, who developed confidence in playing basketball from childhood. When he joined the NBA, he was confident enough to achieve the best results, since he had developed the art from his childhood days. You will need to be confident in yourself before you can achieve your set objectives.

# Seven Ways to Develop Confidence with the Right Mindset

There are several ways of avoiding a bad mindset. Some are cheap and easy to implement, but some can be very hard and costly. Here are some practical ways of uprooting a bad mindset that is preventing you from becoming confident and being an "Alpha" man:

### 1. Practice Positive Affirmations

Jimmy Connors once said: "Use it or lose it." As far as your thoughts and mindsets are concerned, the less you exercise your mind, the weaker it becomes. And as the mind becomes weak, it will be prone to be affected by external factors, which will significantly affect your confidence. By using positive affirmations (positive self-talk), you will exercise your mind toward being confident about yourself. It is an effective way of influencing your subconscious mind to be more confident. Positive affirmations are best used with a partner. Since you are not perfect, by including a trusted friend or member of the family, you will benefit from their help as they will remind you when you go astray from your goals. A partner will tell you to uproot the negative mindset if they see it coming back.

## 2. Stop Thinking About Negative Mindsets

Always loop the bad mindset ideas from your mind. Avoid engaging your mind to think about the wrong mindsets. If you think of why you can't be confident, you will forever question your self-worth. This is like meditating or thinking of a particular thing, so repeatedly that it becomes a part of you. The less you think of the limiting beliefs, the more you develop your self-worth. If done over time, you will be able to increase your self-esteem.

## 3. Interrogating Yourself

The best way of avoiding a negative mindset is to challenge it. You can achieve this by continually questioning yourself about the benefits you are deriving from the limiting mindset. This should be done regularly, so that eventually, you will find yourself completely eliminating the limiting mindsets that affect your confidence.

## 4. Keep the Right Company

To develop your confidence, you should try hanging out with confident men. Transference of spirit will happen when you hang around highly confident people. You will be able to copy what they are doing, and in a short while, and with practice, it will become part of you. The good thing is that with confidence, once you master it, it is impossible to lose it. But again, even on the acquisition, you must practice very often. Experience, they say, is an excellent teacher. But still, you can learn a lot from other people's experiences. This way, you will be able to avoid trying silly things that have already been experienced by your friends, and the repercussions shared with you.

## 5. Seek Excellence

The journey to self-worth requires that you strive to excel in life, rather than being perfect. As we discussed earlier, seeking perfection is the highest confidence killer. On the other hand, excellence is concerned with you giving your best in the tasks that you handle, whether it's work or family, sports, or even schoolwork. Excelling in what you do is a significant boost to your confidence. The secret of excellence is making the most of what you have in your hands. Excellence entails all the choices you make.

### 6. Practice Continuous Improvement

Excelling is the first step in building your self-worth. But after that, you need to continuously excel and improve from your scores from the last count. It is common to find that a costly phone that you purchased recently might be considered old and useless in less than three months. Now back to you, the skills that you have achieved will be outdated in a few months, and this will significantly affect your ability to handle tasks excellently, and consequently, it will affect your self-worth.

For example, social media has recently become a force that shapes personal lives and businesses. The need for social media experts has increased significantly. Many are catching up on this demand and have learned how to be proficient marketers. Therefore, if you are in the marketing profession, you ought to understand the trends in social media marketing and how you can effectively tap into them to increase your business worth. Being on top of the game is a confidence booster. If you don't continuously invest in your personal or professional growth, you run the risk of losing your confidence in the long term.

Conversely, personal growth plays a significant role in boosting your self-confidence. You are way ahead of many by just reading this book. Reading is the most critical and straightforward means of personal growth. By reading books, you can access the minds of many; it also provides you with the luxury of convenience since you can read a book at your own time and pace.

### 7. Visualize

Another way to have a positive mindset is to program your mind through visualization. This is the ability to create a precise and vivid mental image of what you want in life. Create a clear mental picture of yourself performing at your optimum level in any given situation, and visualize it turning out precisely the way you want it to. That way, your confidence levels will increase, since in these visualizations you will consider yourself worthy and contributing to the world positively.

Therefore, we have seen that maintaining a positive mindset and avoiding limiting beliefs is the key to developing self-worth or self-confidence. Positivity is the act of looking at life or the things that happen in your life from a positive perspective.

Maintaining a positive mindset does not mean that you are blind to the negativity that exists in the world. It just means dwelling on the possible or actual good things that can emanate from events, actions, situations, or people. In this section, you have learned how limiting beliefs set the course for your life. What you believe permeates every part of your adult life.

## Mindset Self-Test

To establish whether you are in the right state of mind to handle what life throws at you, you need to assess yourself by asking yourself these questions:

- ✔ Do you have peace of mind?
- ✔ Are you in control of your own life?
- ✔ Do you plan your life well?
- ✔ Do you know how to achieve your full potential?
- ✔ Do you like yourself?
- ✔ Are you concerned about what people may think of you?
- ✔ Are you willing to let bygones be bygones and make changes in your life?
- ✔ Do you expect the best of yourself?
- ✔ Do you regularly practice positive thinking and positive affirmations?
- ✔ Are you destined for success?
- ✔ Are you continuously improving and growing toward your potential?

The questions above will help you to program your mind and even let you know what to think. You are a result of everything you have believed in until now. What you will grow into in the future will ultimately be the result of the content in your mind.

The law of belief states that whatever you believe with feeling becomes your reality, and if you wish to change your reality, you must change your beliefs about yourself first. Additionally, the law of expectation states that whatever you expect with confidence becomes your self-fulfilling prophecy, and for this reason, you must assume the best from others and every situation. Lastly, the law of attraction states that you inevitably attract into your life the people and circumstances that harmonize with your dominating thoughts. To attract different people or situations, you have to change the way you think.

Thus, nobody remains the same for an extended period. You are continually changing in the direction of your dominant thoughts and objectives. You should keep in mind the kind of person you would like to be and the goals you want to accomplish. To develop self-worth, you have to let go of the past. You have to develop new habits and patterns of thinking about yourself. This is done by thinking, talking, and acting in a manner that is consistent with the person you wish to be in the future, with the attributes and characteristics that you would like to adopt.

## Mental Toughness: The Zero F*cks Method

Mental toughness is your ability to deal with pressures, stressors, and challenges and to get the best possible results, despite the circumstances that you might find yourself in. It is also defined as the ability to rise after failures and setbacks, and the resolve to spot and take hold of the opportunities that come up.

Also, mental toughness can be defined as a "character in action." This definition was coined by the famous football coach, Vince Lombardi. Mental toughness is essential because it compensates for the lack of skill, natural ability, and strength. You have often heard it said that the people at the top in any field whatsoever are not the most talented; they are those who stayed and kept at it despite the challenges they faced. Mental toughness prevents you from becoming a quitter. In the documentary *Pumping Iron* (1977), Arnold Schwarzenegger says that you must go on and on, not caring what happens. This resolve is what gets an athlete through the competition in a marathon—you must keep running until you get to the end.

Therefore, whatever you call it—balls, guts, wits, or will—this is what we are calling "mental toughness." The question now is: how do you become mentally healthy and tough?

If you ask around, many coaches, athletes, and corporate leaders will tell you that mental toughness is inborn or developed in the earlier stages of life, depending on the environment a child grows up in. It is challenging to transform people, but with the realization that you are capable of improving the various aspect of your life, this should be followed with the utmost optimism.

## Skills That Define a Mentally Tough Man

Mentally tough people quickly rise to positions of influence and power in business, leadership, sports, and even in life. Observing them keenly, experts have outlined some skills common in all of them.

These defining skills include but are not limited to:

- **A hyper-focus.** This is the ability to perform at peak levels with ease without giving in to distractions and with a clarity of mind. This is called "being within the zone."
- **A winning mindset.** A winning mindset is an attitude that you must win or at least operate at the maximum possible efficiency level, maintaining consistency. To do this, you must have a strong belief and faith in your field of expertise and skills despite the challenges presented to you.
- **Willpower.** As pointed out earlier, willpower combines effort, intention, and courage. The aim is the "will" in

willpower. It is the insistence on staying on the same task until all the work is done. The effort you put into doing something is the power. It propels you into achieving what is required of you despite the challenges you encounter. Courage is the readiness to bear up all the fear and other emotions that you need to accomplish the task.

- **Composed.** A mentally tough person has to keep calm under pressure. As the situation heightens and everyone else is freaking out, the individual remains calm, takes time to assess the situation, and then makes the best possible move. You must stay engaged in the case no matter how high the pressure rises.

- **Lose well.** Along with the mindset of a winner is the ability to accept that the performer is capable of failure. Sometimes, even with the highest focus and costly investment of skills and resources, you can fail to meet the set objective. However, the trick lies in your ability to extract lessons and values from each experience and to channel them into the next trial, for continued success.

- **Own up.** To develop mental toughness, you need to own up to every situation, both the good and the bad. A mentally healthy person is ready and willing to take up that responsibility and pressure. You believe that whatever the challenges and the odds, you must come up with a solution. In case of failure, you will take stock, evaluate your steps to see where you went wrong, gather lessons from it, and then move on past it. You know how to overcome negative emotions and thoughts effectively.

- **Preparation.** Preparedness involves lots of planning. A good man will plan early enough. You will also create a backup plan that can be activated if, indeed, the original plan fails or it just will not work. Planning and preparation of this nature allow you to remain at ease, regardless of the situation.

In addition, the task itself can be fully recovered and completed, without having to return to the starting point. What's more, your spirit is not crushed, and the performance rhythm is not affected much by the perceived loss and failure.

- **Ready to take on the challenge.** A mentally tough person does not whimper. You do not whine. Whatever comes your way, you readily welcome it. Be it having to stay up late to work on some project, be it having to take on more people for training, be it running several extra miles. Whatever it is, you have a "bring it on" attitude, and this produces exposure, experience, and success.
- **Stress optimization.** This is the ability to manage pressure and stress during any event, without any anxiety, fear, or doubt—or at least maintaining your performance undeterred by them. An individual who has learned how to optimize stress will take advantage of a stressful environment and come up with results that others could not have presented under similar conditions.
- **Stretch out the limits.** This is your ability to exact maximum physical effort even in the face of mental and physical stress. You could be in pain or physical discomfort and commit yourself to give the best performance irrespective of the situation at hand. We have seen athletes in severe physical pain go on to finish the race on the tracks.

We have seen above the skills that you need to develop, to claim that you are a mentally tough man. Now, we look at the methods used to achieve mental toughness. Below are the "no f*ck" approaches or habits that you should practice daily to become a mentally tough person:

# Routine Habits of Mentally Tough Men

If you are a mentally tough man, there is a high chance that you were not born tough. You have developed these critical habits and have been practicing them every day, thus setting you apart from other men. These habits are discernible in the way you approach life and the challenges that come to you. A mentally tough man's methods are usually different from the approach of an average man.

As Henry Ford of Ford Motors once put it: "Failure is simply the opportunity to begin again, this time more intelligently." Once you have identified the mistakes that prevent you from succeeding, you will need to develop the right mental attitude to help you navigate through failure and to overcome challenges and differing opinions, and the bad habits that stifle you.

Here are some no f*ck habits that you need to practice daily to develop the mental strength and toughness that you require:

- **Practice gratitude.** As a mentally healthy person, you will count your blessings every day, rather than your problems, to help keep your life in perspective. The "attitude of gratitude" brings the joy that eliminates all negative feelings, and elevates your moods, in readiness for the tasks at hand.
- **Take on challenges.** To a mentally tough person, a challenge is only an opportunity to become stronger. With each victory, you become more confident and better at what you are doing.
- **Maintain healthy boundaries.** Emotional, social, and physical boundaries create the room a tough-minded person needs to grow. Even though saying "no" might disappoint you if you are trying to get past the limits, you are happy to take that risk, for the sake of securing success in the future.
- **Maintain personal power.** A strong person does not allow a negative person to exert any control or influence. You are also not willing to use other people as excuses for why you are being held back or dragged down; you take full responsibility for your actions.
- **Only concentrate on things you have power over.** Mentally tough people know the value of being continually effective and productive in their roles. This can be achieved only when you

focus on the things you can control, rather than wasting precious time thinking about current or future storms that you have no control over. You will expend energy in preparing for and responding to something that happens, rather than in trying to prevent it from happening.

For instance, if the country expects to go into a recession, you don't go about trying to prevent it; it would be a complete waste of time. Instead, you work on managing your organization and planning on the response the company will give when the recession is here. Will production decrease? How will that affect the market? A stable mind will think about those issues.

- **Make peace with the past.** The past is only essential to a tough-minded person for its lessons. You reflect on it so you can learn from it, not regret your actions or those of others. You do not hold grudges either.
- **Learn from mistakes.** Instead of beating yourself up because of an error, a mentally healthy person will focus on the lessons learned. You will take full responsibility for your behavior and choose to move forward, positively.
- **Take calculated risks.** Each decision a mentally tough person makes must be backed by logic so that each risk taken is calculated for its possible pay off and losses. As such, you are willing to step out of your comfort zone to look for non-traditional opportunities and solutions that will propel you to success.
- **Have alone time.** Any successful person will tell you of the value of alone time. When you are left alone to your thoughts, you can meditate, journal, plan, and reflect. Some time of solitude is essential for any growing and innovative mind.
- **Take full responsibility.** As mentioned in a previous point, as a mentally tough person, you will take charge of your life. You do not wait for opportunities to be handed to you, nor do you sit around whining about what should have been or what is owed to you. You go out and make it happen.

- **Persevere.** Strong people are believers of the fact that good things take time, and that they are worth waiting for. You will be persistent and patient as you strive to achieve particular milestones in your life journey.
- **Be realistic in your optimism.** Mentally tough people are not daydreamers. You refuse to be put down by pessimistic opinions and predictions, but still, will not allow yourself to be overconfident.
- **Allow discomfort.** Pain is a necessary part of the process, and a mentally tough person is not afraid to experience some. It may mean getting overly tired or resisting the urge to be gratified instantly. This requires a great deal of self-discipline to endure the discomfort.
- **Work on unhealthy habits.** As a mentally tough person, you will not allow your unhealthy habits to get in the way of your success. You understand that the mind has the capacity to become the worst enemy to your success. Therefore, you are continually working against overindulging in food, your hot temper, hitting the snooze button, watching mind-altering films, and other negative behaviors that limit success.
- **Use your mental capacity wisely.** As a mentally tough person, you will not complain about things that you cannot change, or keep rehashing something that happened in the past. You know better than to devote your energy to activities and tasks that are unproductive. Your limited resources, like time and energy, are used sparingly and in the right manner.

# Five Self-Discipline Habits for Daily Improvement

In the previous section, we have explored why self-discipline may be lacking. It is a quality that must be acquired first of all by assessing yourself and then practicing the habits that will improve your self-discipline. Since self-discipline is an excellent quality, you should not wait for it to come naturally, because it won't. Drop all your excuses and practice self-discipline habits daily.

Start by identifying your objectives and goals, as well as determining why you wish to get rid of all the wrong behaviors. Avoiding excuses is among the many habits that you should practice daily to become a disciplined man.

Below is a detailed description of the five self-discipline habits that you should practice daily:

    **1. Take action**. Don't wait for the right time—it is common to come across advice that tells you to do something when it feels right and stop when you don't feel like doing it. It is said that you should follow your gut. Unfortunately, this is based on emotions, which are often unstable and highly unpredictable. Every man has a rollercoaster of emotions. Developing self-discipline is about learning how to get past the blockade that you create, like waiting for the right time to do something.

As described earlier, self-discipline is what keeps you focused on your goals even when you no longer feel enthusiastic. This means that emotions shouldn't be a determining factor on whether you will get started at something or not. As such, you are waiting for the right feeling or time, and this is a wrong approach to develop all the self-discipline that you need in life.

Choosing to work or not to work on a task based on the comfort it offers is the wrong approach to doing anything, and it is a tactic that can prevent you from gaining self-discipline.

If you are of the mindset that you should wait for the right time and emotion to do something, counter that by revisiting your "Why?". Of course, when you were developing your list of reasons for pursuing a goal, you never factored your emotions into that, so why should they be a determinant factor when it comes to getting things done? But how can you overcome the habit of waiting for the right feeling and time? By taking action, even if it is uncomfortable to do so.

**2. Drop your habit of making excuses.** Next, you need to discard your unhealthy behavior of making excuses for delaying a task. This has everything to do with procrastination. You cannot go far in your quest to build your self-discipline if you continuously procrastinate. The reason you've been struggling over the years to achieve your goals is probably that you make excuses for not starting (which amounts to procrastination).

Let me give you an example of the form that excuses take. "I won't be able to go for a jog because my jogging partner will not come," or "I won't go to the gym for 30 minutes today because I want to go for one-hour next time." Well, all these are excuses. However, if you want to transform yourself into a version that gives no excuses, you will need to be very honest with yourself to determine the real reason why you don't want to do something that needs to be done to achieve your goal.

For instance, if you come up with an excuse like, "I won't go out for a run now since it is freezing outside," then you should be honest with yourself and state the real reason for not jogging. Tell yourself, "I am not going jogging because I am feeling lazy and lack the will to do something healthy."

Nobody will admit to being lazy. That's why this realization will push you out of your self-defined comfort zone of laziness—to prove to yourself that you are not lazy. With time, it will be easy to transform your life when you stop giving excuses for your inability to take action.

**3. Develop an action plan and take action.** This is a habit that you need to develop and practice daily. To develop self-discipline, you will have to work on your personal goals by preparing an action plan for them. Here is how to go about it:

✔ Make your action plan. You can create a tabular action plan or use Excel or MS Word to make one. Find out what steps you need to carry out and in what order they must be performed to do what needs to be done to achieve a particular goal.

Make sure to add essential columns or sections, such as "action to be taken," "time to start the task," "potential problems I could face," "strategies I can adopt for overcoming issues," and "progress report." Next, you need to fill the columns with appropriate content.

✔ Prepare yourself to take action. Once you have filled in the information required to achieve a goal, next is to take action. But before you do that, ensure to go through the document to "absorb" everything that's in it. You should also use this review to identify any flaws in the document, and if you find any, ensure to make the necessary changes.

Next, you need to prepare yourself to take action. In this case, action refers to the steps to be taken to achieve your objectives. For instance, your efforts could include such activities as finding a good yoga class and enrolling in one to start your journey to losing weight with yoga—if that's what you want to achieve. And as you do this, you should let your action plan guide you to action. But if the action plan is not sufficiently detailed so that it has the specifics or even the smallest of details, you can get someone to help you come up with ideas for taking action.

✔ Anticipate problems that may occur and find solutions. You need to consider any potential issue(s) that you are likely to face when working on your action plan and devise strategies that will help you to overcome such issues.

For example, if you worry that you'll switch off the alarm when it rings at 5 am and drift off to sleep again, then a potential problem could be "I will probably fall asleep." Then identify any workable solution that could help you to tackle this issue. For instance, you could ask your partner or your roommate to wake you up and ensure that you don't go back to sleep. You could have an accountability partner who ensures you follow your action plan. They could call you at your exercising time and keep ringing until you actually wake up. Think of similar strategies like these to instill respect in your action plan.

✔ Regularly review your plan. You cannot know how well you are doing if you don't track your progress. This means that you won't be able to tell whether you are really following your action plan.

Therefore, it is important that you make the necessary plans to know how well you are performing with regard to following your action plan. For instance, if you wanted to lose weight (say 15 pounds in two months), you will need to determine how often you will weigh yourself to determine your progress. If you notice any flaws in your action plan, this is the best time to fix that. This will increase your chances of following the procedure and nurturing your self-discipline.

✔ Never repeat mistakes. You are bound to make mistakes along the way. That is okay. Never put yourself down, criticize, or hate yourself upon making a mere mistake. All you need to do is to get up, inspire yourself, and keep pushing. Research shows that when you make a mistake, you are likely to shut down or attempt to solve the problem. If you concentrate on your mistakes and struggle t0 correct them, you are most likely to succeed, as opposed to overlooking your flaws or ignoring them altogether.

✔ When you discover your mistake, take some time to reflect on the mistakes as objectively as possible and avoid blaming yourself or criticizing yourself for any wrongdoing. You want to encourage yourself into action, not put yourself down for your flaws. Reflect on the positives and the benefits that will come with nurturing self-discipline. This will give you a glimpse of the bigger picture, hence increasing your chances of feeling motivated to action, as opposed to feeling bad for making mistakes.

**4. Practice overcoming temptations.** As you work toward building self-discipline, you should anticipate facing many "temptations." Changing yourself from the person that you were in the beginning—a person who lacked self-discipline—to one who has excellent self-discipline, is going to take some time and will have a steep learning curve.

You shouldn't expect to move from one end to the other end of the spectrum instantly without facing any temptations to go back to the habits that you are so used to.

Here are a few strategies on how to overcome temptations and stay committed to your goal:

✔ Detach yourself from the attractions that lead to temptations.

✔ Envisage yourself resisting temptation.

✔ Weigh instant gratification against the long-term consequences.

✔ Keep yourself busy with important stuff to avoid falling into temptation.

**5. Inspire and develop yourself.** Self-discipline is not only created by eliminating temptations from your life; making the right decisions; following your action plans; and dumping excuses. There's something else you need to do as well: nurture yourself and keep yourself motivated.

Gaining self-discipline can be quite challenging, mainly if you are not used to it. You'll make mistakes in the beginning and probably even consider giving up. But since this mostly happens when you don't encourage yourself, you need to come up with creative strategies that you can follow to keep yourself motivated as you work toward transforming your self-discipline.

Here are some sure ways of getting yourself inspired:

✔ Compliment yourself every day.

✔ Take good care of yourself.

✔ Get enough sleep.

✔ Exercise regularly.

# Power Goals: Thinking Long Term for Success

To be successful in life, you must create a clear vision of what you want in life. Set clear goals. From the previous chapters, you have learned about ways of eliminating limiting beliefs. Now you can firm up your personal goals and bring them to life in a way that will register in your unconscious mind and help it happen.

Having a clear image of your goals and objectives into the future will inspire you and keep you focused on doing everything necessary to achieve the goal. This last section of this book will guide you through:

- Why setting goals is key to long term success.
- What works well in setting goals?
- You will learn the five conditions necessary for successful goals.
- You will learn how to make your goals compelling.
- You will learn how to install your goals for long-term success.

**Set Your Goals**

You should set your goals the right way for success. There is a proper way, and there is a wrong way of setting your goals. The right approach should be the SMART way because it allows you to plan, act, and analyze the progress you have made.

You are more likely to succeed in life if you are good at analyzing your progress and keeping track of things that you are supposed to achieve to succeed.

The journey to success will always start with goal setting. These goals will become the central focus of your life. You should choose as few goals as possible, since the more goals you set, the more it will take you to accomplish each.

Because you need to limit your attention to a few goals as possible, you'll undoubtedly have to give up working on other, less important goals. If you fear doing so, you need to ask yourself if spreading yourself thin until now has helped you to achieve anything in life.

**How to Set the Right Goal**

The goal or goals you choose to focus on have to be so important that they can transform your life. They also need to provide more benefits than neglecting your less vital goals. In other words, as an example, you have to feel good forgoing or delaying becoming a great golf player and going to the gym to develop a six-pack in exchange for moving into your dream house.

**Common Transformational Goals**

**1. Getting in shape.** This includes: losing weight, exercising more, replacing bad habits with healthy ones. If your long-term well-being is in danger, no other goal is as important as following your doctor's orders. Forgo any other aspirations and make it your top priority.

**2. Building a business, advancing your career, or rebranding yourself.** This includes learning skills and acquiring the credentials that are needed to change your occupation.

**3. Finding a significant other, starting a family, taking care of your children, and other goals related to relationships.** Just like taking care of your health, this can sometimes be more crucial than any other purpose. Saving your marriage is more important than developing your career.

**4. Learning a skill or developing a trait that will produce a profound change in your life or give you more opportunities.** This could include: eliminating procrastination from your life, learning a foreign language, overcoming shyness, becoming a professional public speaker, or overcoming a paralyzing phobia.

**5. Lifestyle goals, like traveling, buying a house and moving to your dream location.** Ensure that you can't imagine your life without making this goal or goals come true. This is imperative; if you don't think of your goal as a necessity in your life and an absolute must, you won't achieve it.

When I set a goal to become a successful entrepreneur, it wasn't just a wish. There was no possible scenario in which I wouldn't eventually own a profitable business. I was unable to imagine myself working for somebody else.

If you don't have such a deep conviction and desire for the goal or goals you want to achieve, reconsider them. The entire strategy is based on the assumption that you'll either eventually make it happen or die trying (and "eventually" here means that you'll try over and over, even if it's going to take you decades).

You must set clear goals, since they give you direction. When you know what your goals are, you will see the path you have to follow to get there—and you have something to aim for, so you can make corrections if you get blown off your path. Having a sense of purpose is a fundamental human need. Without this, you become unhappy. With setting goals, you will be more flexible and resilient and will be able to cope with changing conditions as you continuously develop.

### How to Select the Goals to Pursue

What happens when you have several goals to pursue, and you are not sure which goals should be dropped and which should wait? There are various techniques that you can use to decide. Below are some:

- **Try flipping a coin.** This technique sounds ridiculous, but it should be approached with an open mind. If you need to decide between two goals, assign goals to each side of the coin and flip it. You'll know which objective is closer to your heart before the coin even lands, because you'll find yourself rooting for it. Pay attention to that emotional response that occurs while you're waiting to see the outcome of the coin toss.

    If you don't have a coin nearby, use an online randomizer, or take two pieces of paper, write down the goals and ask another person to choose one of them without showing them the answers. Again, pay attention to what you are hoping the result will be.

    This approach often works better than analyzing each goal and trying to make a logical decision. It could be because when it comes to setting goals that matter most to you, your gut usually knows best.

- **Think about your most critical values.** Another technique that can help you narrow down your list of goals or prioritize them is to think about your key benefits.

For me, one of my top values is personal freedom; hence my goal was to become a successful entrepreneur.

What is it for you? Is the current state of things preventing you from fully embracing your most crucial values in your everyday life?

For example, if excitement is one of your top values, but you work in a soul-sucking corporation, it will clash with your values for the rest of your life until you do something about it. This indicates that finding a more exciting job might be a good goal to choose as your primary objective.

- **Goals that you can't wait to achieve.** It's generally easy to assess whether somebody cares about something if one looks at their patience for it. If you have a history of giving up after experiencing the first failure, the chances are good that the goal you've chosen is not your priority. On the other hand, if you refuse to give in (even when everybody around you doubts in your ability to succeed), it's an indicator that you're working on the right goal.

Now you know how to set the right goals and which goals to drop. The next step is how to prioritize the goals and how to make sure they're realistic for you. Here, the two crucial questions to ask yourself are "when" and "how" to start.

Before starting the journey to success, and working toward the set goals, you should ask yourself the following questions:

1. **Will the prevailing negative circumstances pose a challenge?** More often than not, you probably won't regret starting sooner rather than later. However, in some instances, waiting might be a more reasonable option.

**2. Have you slept on the job?** Many books will teach excitedly about how you should start it now, right away, with no thought on your part. I've found from my personal experience that it's helpful to sleep on any new goal you have chosen, before taking action.

First, the next morning you'll probably see it from a slightly different perspective, which might give you better ideas on how to proceed. There will be more logic involved in your thought processes and it won't be mostly from your emotional side. Second, if you're not even half as fired up as you were the day before, chances are it was only a spur-of-the-moment idea that doesn't lend itself to a long-term plan.

**3. Are you okay with the dark side of working toward accomplishing this goal?** This is the final question you should ask yourself before commencing to pursue your goals. When you're excited about setting a new purpose and changing your life, it's easy to fall victim to confirmation bias, in which you exclusively seek information that confirms your beliefs, while rejecting alternative or contrary knowledge.

# Bonus – Top Ten Tips to Be a Confident Man

### 1. Believe That You CAN Make Good Decisions

The key to self-confidence and self-esteem is to believe that you *can* make those good decisions. Approaches based on mindfulness, focusing on the moment and positive affirmations that you can do it, all encourage a belief in yourself.

### 2. Tune the Negativity Out

In conjunction with the first tip, you must learn to tune negativity out. Be mindful of what has happened previously but keep an eye on the here and now—you can choose not to listen to ugliness and negativity from others, and from within yourself too.

### 3. Embrace and Learn from Mistakes

Everyone has made mistakes, but there is no shame in it. Push embarrassment to one side and embrace those mistakes; ask yourself what you learned from making them.

### 4. Focus on the Good

You must focus on your personal, physical, and intellectual assets when you review yourself. There must be positive things that you can say; nobody's life is all negative!

### 5. Practice Gratitude

This will positively and directly impact your self-esteem. What you are grateful for? What are the good things in your life? Do this while using mindfulness—you might be surprised at the answers.

### 6. Change Your Mental Self-Talk

Look in the mirror; look hard at yourself and then say something positive about your body, mind, personality, feelings, et cetera. If you can't, you need to switch off the "tape" of negative self-talk and turn on that positive one.

### 7. Change is Constant – Accept and Embrace It

We all change all of the time and what you see of yourself today will be different tomorrow, even if it is a minor change. Ask yourself what you are doing to bring about positive changes. Are you working hard on your body, mind, and spirit?

### 8. You ARE Worthy of Feeling Happiness – Accept It!

Happiness is an important part of life, but you won't attract success unless and until you believe that you are worthy of that happiness. There is a big difference between deserving happiness and being worthy of it—when you are worthy, you can absorb that happiness completely into your being.

### 9. Be Aware of Self-Care

Self-care is an important part of life. Whether it is through physical activity, body-building, diet, even personal grooming and taking care of your mental health. Invest the resources and the time into self-care and bring about positive changes and wellness.

### 10. Embrace Imperfections

Nobody is perfect, no matter how much they think they are. Every flaw you identify in yourself is likely one shared by other men—but ask yourself this—are the flaws really all that bad? Can you accept them as part of who you are? Your imperfections are a part of who you are. Embrace them!

# Conclusion

Now that you have read the book, followed through the exercises provided, and identified what you need to increase your self-worth, it is time to go and practice!

Start adopting the simple strategies recommended here, and you will gradually see the benefits. As you watch these benefits accrue, you will develop a positive attitude toward change, and thus your self-esteem will improve.

Although it is important to note that these changes do not happen overnight, you should be patient enough and understand that it takes time to be the person you desire to be—but the results are so worthwhile.

As your self-esteem and self-confidence increase, you will experience increased growth that will lead to greater happiness in life. Getting started in the journey to self-worth is the hardest part; therefore, I suggest that you apply the tips presented in this book immediately. The tips are proven, and they work, but remember—they may not work for everyone. The suggestions offered in this book should also not be applied all at once. Create a plan that will help you to logically and sequentially implement the tips gradually.

The most important part is to make an effort to transform yourself, and you will feel the transformation taking place sooner than you envisaged. Try spending a few days working on one or two tips. Once you are in sync with the process, then try another one until they all become second nature. Your confidence will increase, and you will feel good about yourself and your life.

Additionally, keep a confidence journal. Just practice writing down ten things that you feel confident about. If done daily, it will change the way you think and feel about everything. I recommend you write your journal just before you go to bed. This way, the things you have written will flow into your subconscious mind as you sleep. You will not only wake up more confident, but you will also be happier with your achievements of the previous day, and you will have motivation and a clear plan for the next day.

In a nutshell:

✔ You hold the power to transform how you feel.

✔ Never feel bad for putting your needs first.

✔ You will not be selfish if you consider your needs first.

✔ Always try to be gentle on yourself; there is only one version of you in this world. So, take good care of it.

✔ Never hate the skin you are in.

Self-confidence is not engraved in men; thus, it can be enhanced or lost at any time. It is mostly affected by external factors that will make you believe that you don't have control over them.

Finally, confidence is within every man, but sometimes when the world is throwing you all manner of challenges, it can fade. Apply the tips discussed in this book when you are feeling less confident. It is not hard to acquire confidence, but if you don't have enough of it, succeeding in life can be difficult. You need the desire or drive to achieve confidence as a man and the persistence to stay at it until you get it. Your ideas, reflection, and thoughts can build your self-confidence, but you have to be aware of these to reach their full benefit.

By reading *Self-Confidence for Men: Unleash the Lion within and See How Your Mental Toughness, Self-Esteem, Mindset, Self-*

*Discipline, and Dating Life Transforms,* you've already taken the first step on your journey. We hope you take full advantage of this book's structure, as you embrace your inner strength and develop your self-worth. Good luck!

# Sources

1. Burton, K., & Platts, B. (2012). *Confidence for Dummies.* Wiley.
2. Schuster, S. (2018). *22 Habits of People With Low Self-Esteem.* The Mighty. Retrieved 11 February 2020, from https://themighty.com/2018/10/low-self-esteem-habits/.
3. Goldsmith, B. (2010). *100 Ways to Boost Your Self-confidence: Believe in Yourself and Others Will Too.* Career Press.
4. McGee, P. (2012). *Self-confidence: The Remarkable Truth of Why a Small Change Can Make a Big Difference.* Capstone.
5. Smith, E. (2018). *How Self-doubt Manifests in Men Versus Women.* Devex. Retrieved 12 February 2020, from https://www.devex.com/news/how-self-doubt-manifests-in-men-versus-women-92506.
6. Pollack, B. (2019). *Male Body Image and Body Dissatisfaction.* Mirror Mirror Eating Disorder Help. Retrieved 13 February 2020, from https://www.mirror-mirror.org/body-image-men.htm.
7. Blumer, C. (1934). *Discipline and Self-Discipline. The Australian Quarterly, Vol. 6 (Issue 23),* 116. Australian Institute of Policy and Science. Retrieved 13 February 2020, from, **https://doi.org/10.2307/20629153**.
8. Bale, C. (2016). *From Shy Guy To Ladies Man – Memoirs Of A Male Seducer.* Ronlif Publishers.

Check out another book by Kory Heaton

www.ingramcontent.com/pod-product-compliance
Lightning Source LLC
Chambersburg PA
CBHW070048230426

**43661CB00005B/812**